"Reading this book feels like sitting across from Dunk with a glass of premium whiskey in your hand, listening to him tell stories that make you laugh, then tear up… then stop and think. With honesty, wit (no one on this planet makes me laugh harder than Duncan) and a deep love for Jesus, Duncan invites us to imagine a church where grace is not just preached, but practiced. It's a messy, beautiful, glorious and different take on doing church. This isn't a how-to manual or a polished theological tome… it's a raw, refreshing, spirit-led conversation about the messy, mystical, and beautiful possibility of encountering God in real time."

—**Lucy Holmes**
Radiohost on Melbournes 89.9 The Light and
The Lucy and Kel Podcast.

"I have known my friend Duncan Robinson for over two decades. We have spent countless hours together in ministry, martial arts, and life. In short, Duncan is the 'real deal.' He is funny and talented, but most of all, he is passionate about an authentic relationship with Jesus.

In *Full Phoenix Rising*, Duncan recalls powerful, personal stories and integrates deep theology toward carving a path of following Christ. As you read, join him in his journey of seeing the weaknesses of a polished, perfect Christian life and the blessings of a more broken but biblical way of finding and following Jesus. So don't be surprised by the story of helping a former burlesque dancer leading a Bible study, the pain of closing a church plant, and the unforeseen success of being a popular radio talk show host. Duncan is just on an adventure of *Real-Time Grace at the Speed of Jesus*. If you want the same for yourself, then read this book and invite Jesus to take you on your own adventure with Him!"

—**Dr. Joshua Anderson**
Director, Grand Canyon Theological Seminary at
Grand Canyon University
Phoenix, Arizona, USA

"Duncan's book is relevant, humorous, and deeply grounded yet refreshingly free of ego. He connects the timeless way of Jesus to the complexities of modern life and the realities of the local church like no one else I know, making this a timely and essential read for anyone feeling busy or trying to control their life but feeling perilously out of control."

—James Dawson
Lead Pastor Anchor Church Northern Beache

"Duncan is a gift to the church! Full Phoenix Rising is full of his best stories, laugh out loud church moments and insights into the heart of Gods grace. Duncan helps us to take God seriously and ourselves not too seriously. That can only help us find a life giving faith."

—Tim Giovanelli
Senior Pastor Manly Life Church.

"There is a wildness to Jesus and his radical message. That's what I love about Duncan Robinson's *Full Phoenix Rising*. We hear and meet Jesus in the equally wild, messy, and raw stories from Duncan's life. If you want a fresh perspective of what an out-of-left-field unfiltered life with Jesus can look like, then this book is for you."

—Sam Chan
Head trainer and mentor,
EvQ school of evangelism, City Bible Forum
Author of *How to Talk About Jesus (Without Becoming THAT Guy)*

Full Phoenix Rising

Real Time Grace at the *Speed of Jesus*

Duncan Robinson

LUCIDBOOKS

Full Phoenix Rising
Real Time Grace at the Speed of Jesus

Copyright @2025 Duncan Robinson
Published by Lucid Books in Houston, TX
www.LucidBooks.com

All rights reserved. No part of this publication may be reproduced, stored in a retrieval system, or transmitted in any form by any means, electronic, mechanical, photocopy, recording, or otherwise, without the prior permission of the publisher, except as provided for by USA copyright law.

Unless otherwise indicated, scripture quotations are taken from the (NIV) the Holy Bible, New International Version®, NIV®. Copyright ©1973, 1978, 1984, 2011 by Biblica, Inc.™ Used by permission of Zondervan. All rights reserved worldwide. www.zondervan.com The "NIV" and "New International Version" are trademarks registered in the United States Patent and Trademark Office by Biblica, Inc.™

Scripture quotations marked (AMP) are taken from the Amplified Bible. Copyright © 1954, 1958, 1962, 1964, 1965, 1987 by The Lockman Foundation, La Habra, CA. All rights reserved. Used by Permission.

Scripture quotations marked (MSG) are taken from THE MESSAGE, copyright © 1993, 2002, 2018 by Eugene H. Peterson. Used by permission of NavPress. All rights reserved. Represented by Tyndale House Publishers, Inc.

Scripture quotations marked (NIRV) are taken from the New International Reader's Version. Copyright © 1995, 1996, 1998, 2014 by Biblica, Inc.®. Used by permission. All rights reserved worldwide.

ISBN: 978-1-63296-810-4
eISBN: 978-1-63296-811-1

Special Sales: Most Lucid Books titles are available in special quantity discounts. Custom imprinting or excerpting can also be done to fit special needs. Contact Lucid Books at Info@LucidBooks.com

Most book dedications feature people you've never heard of, they are close to the author and played an important part in the crafting of the book. I've done that in the next part with a special thanks. This book I choose to dedicate to you. It takes time and effort to read a book, no matter the length, it is a personal investment on your behalf that is costly. So I want to say thank you.

Without your dedication to reading this, I wouldn't have a dedication to writing. Writing like most art requires a willingness to release what is created to the world. That opens yourself to scrutiny and criticism, it also opens yourself to the possibility of inspiration. My hope and prayer is that you might be more inspired by Jesus (not me) and more transformed by his ever present grace in your life.

So this book is dedicated to you, the reader.

Table of Contents

Introduction	1
How Youth Ministry Led to My Conversion	5
An Ecclesiastical Quibble of Note	11
Think about Church as Time, not Space	21
Top Five Weirdest Church Moments	27
Illegal Basketball Uniforms	33
Learning to Live by Grace	38
Church Planting 101	41
Our Identity In Christ	47
I Am Chosen	52
I Am Beloved	55
I Am Forgiven	60
I Am Set Free	64
I Am Called	69
I Am Serving	73
I Am Reconciling	77
I Am Loving	81
Naked Jim	87

When Do Sinners Stop Sinning in the Company of Jesus?	91
The Reality of Sin and Regeneration	94
Grace, Regeneration, and the Messiness of Church	95
Where Do We Find Grace in Abundance?	96
Grace in the Midst of Trial	97
The Starting Blocks of Grace	99
Some Final Thoughts about Grace	100
The Problem with Church	103
Moving Toward Transformation	105
Pastor of Disaster	107
The Problem with Church Mission	108
Prioritizing the Mission	109
Nomads of Hope	111
Recognizing and Combatting Persistent Restlessness	116
An Undignified Response and Weapons-grade Prayer	121
US Camps Are the Best!	127
A Mighty Red Gum of Faith	133
The Slow Messy Grace of Jesus	139
A Black Sheep Church	145
Closing Thoughts	151
Endnotes	155

Special Thanks

Firstly, a huge thanks to my family who helped to make this happen. Carly, Ruby, and Max who let me retreat to the back office and write away.

To Judy, Zoe, Phil, Jan and Amy who immediately said yes when I needed help to make this happen.

To Matt my neighbour and to my church community who continue to inspire me to live out the two greatest commandments.

Introduction

The title *Full Phoenix Rising* comes from my buddy Lucy who hosts a breakfast radio show in Melbourne. I became friends with her and her cohost Kel on a mission trip to Vietnam. We were in a remote village on the north side of Vietnam raising money for cataract surgeries. Christian Blind Mission (CBM), an organization that partnered with our radio stations, had us staying at a random hotel in a small town that had recently upgraded their internet infrastructure so we could broadcast the incredible work the doctors were doing in this small community.

One night, I was heading out to meet up with the group when I rounded the corner of the hotel to discover that Lucy was being cornered by a Russian mechanic wearing gold hot pants and holding a bottle of vodka. Lucy is blonde and gorgeous, which makes her pretty rare for radio, but she is a flaming white unicorn when you bury her in a remote village in Vietnam. This Russian mechanic must have thought he was dreaming.

Kel was gently trying to explain to the Russian that Lucy wasn't interested in a private party in his room and that we all had some place to be. He wasn't excited by the prospect of Kel, and he certainly wasn't excited by the prospect of me. I arrived and suggested with only two glasses, we couldn't have a drink together; we needed a third. When he retreated to his bedroom, we told Lucy to run. She screamed, "Phoenix Rising" and took off down the corridor.

Our Russian buddy emerged not only with extra glasses but a larger bottle of vodka and photos of the fighter jets he was working on at the secret Russian base that he thought we might be interested in. He became less jovial when he realized Lucy was no longer with us and that he was left staring at two balding middle-aged men. Still, he was undeterred by the notion of having a good time, so he poured us shots and invited us into his bedroom.

Kel and I took a shot, screamed "Dostoevsky," and took off down the hall as fast as we could. Eventually, we all connected back up, had a drink together, and decompressed from the harrowing experience with the drunk hot-pants Russian we had encountered. I asked Lucy what "Phoenix Rising" meant, and she explained that whenever she overcame a challenge or adversity or something difficult, she'd call out "Phoenix Rising" as a kind of a rally cry. I loved it. Having just moved back to Australia from Phoenix, Arizona, and loving the mythical phoenix, I quickly adopted the idiom myself.

Later, I added the idea of "Full Phoenix" to reflect just how bad the situation was: The harder the challenge, the fuller the phoenix. As I reflected on my experience with

INTRODUCTION

Jesus—those moments when grace was truly present in my life—I started to think about the speed at which Jesus moves in our lives and the radical impact of grace, which extends well beyond our first encounters with God. Sometimes our walk with Jesus is messier, slower and funnier than we might first expect. Bob Goff talks about whimsy: "Living a life fully engaged and full of whimsy and the kind of things that love does is something most people plan to do, but along the way they just kind of forget."[1]

The daft conglomeration of mistakes that has led me to this point can only safely be described as full phoenix rising—not a theological framework, not a profound discipleship model, not even a Christian inspirational book. This book is comprised of a random series of events, which convinced me that it is better that I know Jesus. Worse without. Here's my perspective: I am a messy black sheep of a Christian, yet God seems to work through that broken messy Duncan and amidst it all, a movement of Grace propels me through life at the speed of Jesus, in real time.

Full Phoenix Rising is not intended to be a book with an answer, except that I've found Jesus showing up in the weirdest places such as in a cow pat fight in a middle of a field. As you wind your way through the pages of this book, you will encounter a collection of funny stories and some deep thoughts about things that really matter to the future of the church.

Sometimes, we want a well-articulated argument, and God reminds us of Ecclesiastes 7:13, which says, *"Consider the work of God; for who can make straight, what He has made crooked"* (NKJV). What if this crooked story of grace at work is the speed at which the future of church has to move? That is, it's the speed at which we embrace our flaws, not as an excuse, but as an acknowledgment that God works in the humble and faithful, and even in our weakness, we can find the true strength of God. It almost feels a little like Apostle Paul's declaration in 2 Corinthians12:10: *"That is why, for Christ's sake, I delight in weaknesses, in insults, in hardships, in persecutions, in difficulties. For when I am weak, then I am strong."* The good stuff is present in the mess, and this a book about Grace at work in the mess.

How Youth Ministry Led to My Conversion

Everyone has a conversion story—whether it relates to finding Jesus or some other aspect of life. For instance, I'm a recently minted Jiu Jitsu Black Belt, and I mention that multiple times because that's another of my conversion stories. I could tell you more about my Jiu Jitsu conversion experience . . . but that is another story for another time.

Everyone has a moment they can point to that changed them from one kind of person into another. For me the most profound and influential transformation was my conversion to faith in Jesus.

When I was about fourteen years old, I went to a Year 9 Camp with my local church. Ours was a classic Australian church campsite with beds covered in thick vinyl and mattresses filled with hard packed straw for sleeping. The restroom was built entirely out of cinder block—showers, toilets, and sinks (except the doors) were cinder block. The doors were abnormally small and made from recycled miniature blue barn doors. The food hall featured orange plastic chairs and foldable tables. The meeting room was literally a room with a small portable sound system in the corner.

If I had to characterize the accommodation, I would say that it was most likely juvenile justice system chic. Not major crimes, but the level that says, "We are going to have a crack at reforming these kids and hope they turn out well, but they need to know we're not spending any money on them or their accommodation."

That was my first camp. I was from a private all-boys school, and I was there because girls were there. I still wasn't entirely sure what I wanted to do with girls—just knew I needed to be around them. My life at that time was 90 percent dominated by Nintendo 64s, but I had just enough time to take on a new learning project.

We did typical church camp stuff. We sang together, ate together, and sat in small groups. And someone patiently explained Jesus to us, until we had free time, and then we all played together. Honestly it was great; there weren't any screens, and we did bushwalks.

Looking back, I think that our camp experience would have been considered an Occupational Health and Safety (OH&S) nightmare. One night, we had a massive pillow fight, and I'm pretty sure several of the guys sustained concussions. Today, the leadership would be fired by church's eldership board and make headlines on some local news channel.

But that pillow fight was all-time epic. Close to 150 teenagers had pillows tightly wedged into the ends of their pillowcases. For those who aren't down with physics, force is calculated as the mass of an object multiplied by acceleration: $F = m * a$.

The thing is, we were generating a centrifugal force, which requires us to factor in the radius and the angular velocity. Assuming that a teenager can generate somewhere close to 90 rpms of angular velocity, when you compact a pillow down to about a radius of 20 cm, you can make something that might initially weigh a kilogram suddenly feel like you are getting hit with a seventeen-kilogram sledgehammer.

The battle was fierce. Initially, it was students versus leaders, then boys versus girls, then just an all-out battle royal. There were casualties; sick bay was overwhelmed. It ended with a glorious run from one of the leaders, Graham, who came storming down the hill and spear-tackled a student to the ground with a thunderous blow. It was worthy of a write-up in the Youth Camp Valhalla Hall of Fame if there were such a thing.

The only event run today that rivals that battle is Kajbe Kan-Kan, a Northern American sacred youth group activity that has surely caused countless rotator cuff injuries. Again . . . a story for another chapter.

Back to my Year 9 Camp. We went caving, and by that, I mean, we put torches on our heads and squeezed into rock holes to see if there were caves. In Australia caves are where all the deadly spiders and snakes have their secret meetings. If you were to pitch a silly idea today, it would be to put kids in overalls, give them torches, and tell them to find holes in the ground in the Australian outback and climb into them. We spent six hours in a field, climbing into holes in the ground and finding underground caves. The only supervisors were twenty-year-old volunteers who were completely clueless and a North American Youth group leader who had a wild dream.

Not a single snake or spider was found, but we had an incredible adventure that day discovering secret caves, then switching off all the torches and being overwhelmed by the suffocating darkness. The darkness was used as an analogy of what it was like to either be in hell or live without Jesus. To be clear, suffocating darkness is an assault on the senses; your eyes cannot process any light, but if you calm down, your other senses kick in and become heightened. Such an experience sits much closer to the origin store of *Daredevil* than it does hell . . . or life without Jesus. What was cool was to see that the smallest light in a darkened room illuminated the whole space, including the couple who were cave kissing in the corner. To be clear it wasn't me, but it helped to unpack a little more about the types of activities females might be willing to participate in. I do wish I had the bold confidence to cave kiss in the dark on a camp with my youth leader no less than six feet away.

However, I was more interested in the processing power of Nintendo's new game architecture. Still the power of light, however small, in a space however large is impressive. In the face of oppressive darkness, the smallest glimmer of hope brings profound perspective.

Which leads me to my final Year 9 Camp OH&S nightmare: the cow-pat fight that convinced me that Jesus was a worthy experience. We went for a walk through the fields to look at cows, which when you are from a city, is a fun experience. Cows are massive, and it's important to put a face to their delicious insides.

We were standing in a field that had recently been occupied by cows, and someone decided to pick up a three-day old patty and launch it like a frisbee toward another youth group student. That kid was shocked. There was a moment of silence for the fallen youth group kid; then an all-out cow-pat fight erupted.

Sidenote: The perfect cow pat for launching isn't a fresh one, you need it to harden a little in the sun, which allows it to stabilize into a disc, a poo frisbee, which allows you to fling it at a person with great accuracy. The goal isn't to throw it like a creme pie into someone's face; think more disc golf. The goal was to tag a person with maximum velocity, using a cow pat, which lends itself perfectly as a frisbee.

So, we waged war: Sides were drawn—guys versus girls as is often the narrative at youth camps. We weren't pulling patties; this was equal opportunity cow pat war. At the end of about two hours, there was not a single soul in that field who wasn't covered in cow poo.

If Dolores the flower lady at my old church had heard about this event, there would have been a formal investigation (more about Dolores later). Half the church would have been sacked. Today, such frivolity would have been talked about in Bible colleges as a barbaric Dark Ages practice. Someone at the Gospel Coalition would write a piece denouncing the practice, citing at least twenty-six reasons why cow pat fights sit outside the gospel.

Tired, stinky, and exhausted, we sat under the shade of a tree carefully removing excrement from our faces. Our youth pastor, Ken, shared Psalm 133 with the guys' small group. He explained that fellowship can feel like a moment when heaven is revealed a little bit. Ken said that when brothers and sisters have a fun, healthy relationship and enjoy one another's company, that truly feels a little like Heaven. He said that the joy we felt in that moment was the kind of joy Jesus wants us to experience with Him. Jesus makes good relationship great. That was one of the all-time great messages, and I am still convinced that those "best day ever" experiences are there to remind you just how good Heaven is. I've been chasing that cow pat high ever since.

An Ecclesiastical Quibble of Note

Amidst the deconstruction movement that has unfolded over the last few years, I have wondered about the shape of the church in the future. I noticed that many people have lost confidence in traditional institutional structures for church and that the great plague of 2020 seemed to serve as a catalyst for questioning matters of faith. Interestingly, N. T. Wright notes:

> Trying to jump from an earthquake, a tsunami, a pandemic or anything else to a conclusion about "what God is saying here" without going through the Gospel story is to make the basic theological mistake of trying to deduce something about God while going behind Jesus' back.[2]

We can look for God at work in the seismic events, and we start to question our faith, but it always needs to start with the Good News of Jesus.

My movement, the Churches of Christ in New South Wales, tries to keep Jesus agile. We don't have giant theological creeds; instead, we have simple sayings such as, "no creed but Christ and the Bible as our guide." It's simple, and I like that catchphrase. For the longest time, I was the prodigal son of multiple church movements. I was saved in a Sydney Anglican Church. I attended a Baptist Bible College. I worked for a Presbyterian Church. I moved to the States and became an ordained Swiss Baptist (Converge) pastor before moving back to Australia to plant a church. Somewhere in there, I also did a City-to-City Church Planting assessment and an A29 Assessment, partnered with a nondenominational charismatic publisher, and then found a crew that was simply Team Jesus.

For the longest time I was frustrated with denominational hurdles that seemed to make Jesus more complex than He needed to be. What I appreciated about deconstruction practices was the way they addressed the questions of what is cultural and what is essential. In my head that felt simple: No creed but Christ and the Bible is my guide. Practically it also requires some reflection on what denominational scaffolding we have put into place and sorting out which things are cultural practices versus Jesus-centric practices.

If deconstruction leads you to the feet of Jesus, there is good in that faith audit. However, if the practice of deconstruction leads you to a place without Jesus, then we might have a real and significant problem. A third century theologian, Cyprian, wrote, "You cannot have God as your Father unless you have the church for your Mother."³ With multiple instances of Scripture (Ephesians 5:25–27 and Revelation 21) pointing to Jesus and the Church being wed, it seems unacceptable to divorce the church and date Jesus.

The relationship between Jesus and His Church led me to ponder the relationship between Yahweh and David. In 2 Samuel 11 David covers his sin by putting Uriah on the front line where he is killed so he can marry Bathsheba. Then a chapter later, Nathan confronts David about his sin, which leads to both repentance and consequences for his actions. Although Yahweh doesn't excommunicate David, He highlights the issues or consequences that will arise, including conflict and war and the death of the child. In 2 Samuel 23, we see the final words of David, which include the following:

> *The Rock of Israel said to me* [David], *"The one who rules righteously, who rules in the fear of God, is like the light of morning at sunrise, like a morning without clouds, like the gleaming of the sun on new grass after rain." Is it not my family God has chosen? Yes, he has made an everlasting covenant with me. His agreement is arranged and guaranteed in every detail. He will ensure my safety and success.*
> —2 Samuel 23:3–5 NLT

He will ensure my safety and success!? In a modern context, David wouldn't make our leadership team; the moment this story with Uriah was discovered, he would be buried. Reconciliation is hard, but Yahweh continues to use David in leadership despite profound failure.

Imagine a church marketing team working overtime to smooth over the situation. The relevant article detailing David's crippling fall. What would the podcast about the rise and fall of David, son of Jesse, look like?

Yahweh doesn't embrace the sin; in fact, there are significant and real consequences. But David remains the king in that brokenness and has real and significant things to offer right up until he dies and then is celebrated. We retroactively apply a grace to David that would not exist in modern times. We no longer function with faulty leaders; instead, we cast them away in shame and move swiftly to what we hope is a safer option.

Yet everyone, everywhere, at all times needs Jesus. The story is as much about the real-time grace of Yahweh as it is about looking upon David with rose-tinted glasses. Jesus does the same: Unskilled workers, a sea of sinners, and some women with undignified backgrounds become the all-star team of evangelism for when He departs.

Jesus moves slowly with real-time grace, with His disciples in close proximity and allows them to make mistakes and coaches them along the way. At no time does He become a raging liberal and depart from truth, but He administers the truth in love. Part of love is real-time grace. Jesus works alongside Judas, equipping and teaching and training him. Jesus doesn't just love John; He loves all his disciples! This means that Jesus is working with a faulty crew of sinners who are making mistakes, missing the point, and failing at critical junctures. Not once does He eject; not once does He give up; not once does He move to plan B.

So why can't we be like this in our churches? Again, I don't mean embracing sin like there aren't consequences but embracing grace like there is always potential for transformation. Rather than committing a barrage of journalistic homicide on our people every time they sin, can we figure out a way to practice grace? I just wonder if there is a church model where grace, redemption, forgiveness, and protection all sit together. It is unlikely to be easy or pretty, but perhaps the next season of church that we attempt will be profoundly grace-filled in real-time.

The last Psalm of David (Psalm 72) ends with these words in verse 19: *"Praise be to the LORD God, the God of Israel, who alone does marvelous deeds. Praise be to his glorious name forever; may the whole earth be filled with his glory. Amen and Amen."*

David would have it no other way than Yahweh. There is a sense that despite what had happened in his life, his last words needed to be a celebration of his might, generosity, and favor for the impoverished and for God's enduring eternal goodness. David's last points celebrate the enduring ways that God has been at work in his own life and present within his community. This makes me think David is flipping gracious about it.

As a teenager, I remember having a church leader explain that I was a black sheep. That leader explained that because I was unpredictable and didn't easily fit into a box, he couldn't use me much. He thought that it was unlikely that I would become a leader. Since that moment, all I wanted to do was serve a black-sheep church; I've been on a mission to lovingly embrace misfits with the real-time grace of Jesus. If we have a "messier" church with a lower bar for participation and if we offer reconciliation and radical practices of love and grace, might we have an altogether messier church who were closer to Jesus?

Yes, nothing will fix the church, but Jesus will transform the church. Could we be both messier and closer while desiring to champion the best in people, to coach real-time and allow mistakes because Jesus did the same with us? Not embracing sin so grace might abound (Paul taught against that option in Romans), but acknowledging the weight of sin, embracing the awe-inspiring grace of God, and championing people toward Jesus who ultimately will redeem us all.

Grace isn't just a saving grace. It's a fuel for day-to-day living. It's a salve for daily accidents. It's justice when things aren't right, and Jesus is so liberal with administering grace that people who don't even know him, experience grace every day.

As I reflect on my own journey of faith, I keep looking for key signposts that marked pivotal experiences. I'm thinking of the grace markers that showed God at work in the mess, and I keep coming back to the ways that grace was at work in my youth group. My youth group experience was wild. Even today, I'm concerned that some incredible story from my early youth group days is going to land someone in some kind of CIA investigation. But my entire youth group experience was built on a simple idea:

- We want you to know you are loved.
- We are committed to being here for you.
- We care about what you are becoming.

These are the same kind of values I have as a parent, but I think it's important to acknowledge it feels cooler when someone closer to your older brother's age is sharing them with you. So twice a week, I'd attend a Bible study where I rarely paid any attention and a Sunday service where we did exactly what every other Lutheran/Evangelical church has done for the last 300 years. We sang, we prayed, and we listened to a message.

The program wasn't the point; the people were. Ken clearly cared about us; he showed up twice a week. He'd come to sporting events. He'd be at all the camps. He was always available to help and to share insights. He was cool; he boxed and listened to cool music. He clearly knew the Scripture inside and out. He sailed from the US to Australia. That blew me away: He sailed to Australia.

We used to load up in the back of his Suzuki 4WD without the roof on and drive down to buy hot chips before doing donuts on some random field and then driving back before my mum saw what we were doing. It was fun—really fun.

I remember the time the church renovated the house where Ken was living, and he had a demolition party. We literally showed up at his house with sledgehammers and busted up walls. We smashed stuff for hours and then went home. That was likely another potential OH&S incident, but it was one of the coolest Friday nights of my childhood—just smashing stuff at the old church house, which was getting demolished the next day.

There's a passage in Matthew 18 that talks about a shepherd looking for the one lost sheep. The shepherd would leave the ninety-nine others and search high and low for the one. I often felt like that's how Ken ran his youth group. It's easy to leave the ninety-nine. They are fine with each other, and the experience is fun; they have experienced people who have been there before and know what to do. But there was always an opportunity to find the one person who was searching. They were invited too.

Churches don't tell you that you don't get to keep your youth pastor forever. No matter how good it is, that person is leaving. I was a youth pastor, and I was the jerk who sowed into a great group of youth, building lifelong friends at three churches and then dumping them. I'm sorry.

Ken is also sorry, so is literally every youth pastor everywhere who left a great program to move onto the next thing. We suck, it hurts, we know. We're sorry. In Scripture, Apostle Paul laments that he couldn't be with his previous churches. He had a burning desire to reach the world with the good news of Jesus, and it took him away from incredible people and incredible friendships. So, for the sake of Christ, he had to be a jerk and say goodbye, and he was sorry.

In our youth group, Ken was replaced with another guy who was nothing like him. The new guy was great for a certain crew and had clearly been hired because he sat more in line with the theological perspectives of the church. The problem was that this new youth pastor led the whole program, and he didn't share the same affection for me that Ken had; it felt like he was looking for white sheep only. Then, we got another new small group leader, Scott, who was like Ken-lite. He was an accountant, which I assumed meant that he had given up on life. That wasn't true. Scott kept the same three principles as Ken had, and I still count him as a friend today.

One of the strengths of the youth group ministry was leadership development. There were always opportunities to apprentice leading stuff, which, by the way, is the best way to share Jesus. Just have a crack; if you mess it up, ask for help. Jesus did that; when the disciples got stuff wrong, he helped them. It's apprenticing, not academic research. Try it out; see if it works; if not, ask for help.

Although I'd been attending our youth group for a while, I still was nowhere near a good kid, but I was hoping to get a chance to lead. However, I regularly missed out on chances to lead. Eventually, I met up with the new youth pastor and asked, "Mate, are you ever going to ask me to lead something?" His response was, "You are a black sheep, Duncan, and I don't really know how to use you."

At the time, his comment felt hurtful. Today, it feels like the most exciting complement. What he wanted was vanilla, predictable, reproducible, and teachable. That is a fair request when you are running a big youth group. The leader needs the Lukes of the world who give orderly accounts to keep everything running smoothly. But friend, that isn't me. I'm a flaming peacock; I'm a bull in a fine China store. I purposely antagonize, frustrate, and think outside the box. Mine is a unique set of skills that might excite Liam Neeson in *Taken*, but in a church searching equilibrium, I would not help.

If you are a young person seeking leadership opportunities, let me say this to encourage you, because I couldn't say this to teenage Duncan: You haven't yet arrived, but your gifts and talents are seen. You are marked with purpose, and you have incredible value. There is an anointing on your life that is far bigger than your tiny youth group. There is a place for the black sheep to do something profound for the kingdom of Jesus, and what you think it might be, may not be what the good king has in store. Patience is the hardest lesson; persevere and build resilience.

Nos are often not-yets in disguise. If you've been told you don't fit the mold, brilliant. I didn't want to be a cookie-cutter Christian in a predictable church, serving neat sandwiches on Sunday. Church is a messy conglomeration of one-of-a-kind brilliant people trying to figure out how to celebrate Jesus together.

Messy weird is good. Black sheep are my sheep. And as Jesus demonstrated with His disciples, He often chooses the misfits, the outcasts, and the unlikely to do incredible things in His kingdom. Just as He chose fishermen, tax collectors, and zealots to carry out His mission, He continues to use ordinary people with extraordinary purpose. Just as in Luke 19:10, Jesus says, *"For the Son of Man came to seek and to save the lost."* He seeks out the lost, the broken, the misfits, and transforms them into instruments of His grace and love, shining brightly in the darkness.

Think about Church as Time, not Space

Recently, Dan, one of our worship leaders, gave a message and referenced *The Sabbath* by Abraham Joshua Heschel, in which Heschel makes the point that church is a religion of time, not space.[4] That is a very big point; technical civilization is a conquest of space, but how do we triumph by sacrificing time to create space?

So, we build, we tunnel, we develop and construct. The result is that we conquer space by sacrificing time. Geo-political conflicts exist with a battle for space, not time. Our goal is to gain power by gaining space and without thought, we will sacrifice time to achieve this.

Dan's point was this: Judaism and Christianity are religions of time. We have significant spaces of worship whether they be a synagogue or cathedral, but they are sanctified by time. That is to say, the process of:

1. Remembering God's promises and provisions
2. The keeping of rituals such as Passover, communion, and baptism
3. Observing festivals, lamentations, and sabbath

These activities sanctify the believer in the space, so effectively the time spent in worship sanctifies the space. No space is holy but is rather made holy by the process of time, which is precisely the point that Abraham Heschel's daughter Susannah makes as she reflects on her father's perspective:

> My father defines Judaism as a religion centrally concerned with holiness in time. Some religions build great cathedrals or temples, but Judaism constructs the Sabbath as an architecture of time. Creating holiness in time requires a different sensibility than building a cathedral in space: We must conquer space in order to sanctify time.[5]

Holiness can only be developed in time. You can take away the Promised Land, and the people of Israel can still be holy; remove the cathedral or the church, and a community can still find a place of holiness. Time requires time to master itself; it has no other master.

In the Bible, no thing or place is holy by itself; not even the Promised Land is called holy. While the holiness of the land and of festivals depends on the actions of the Jewish people, who have to sanctify them, the holiness of the Sabbath, he writes, preceded the holiness of Israel. Even if people fail to observe the Sabbath, it remains holy.[6]

However, we often don't function as a church of time. We become space-oriented regarding the facility, the worship space, the chairs, and the lights and the entrance. We ponder the graphics, the social media, and the digital assets and marketing while forgetting that our greatest cathedral exists in time and that sabbath is its architecture. I don't mean architecture in the sense of the Roman Colosseum or Fallingwater by Frank Lloyd Wright, but something that requires maintenance to weather time. Sabbath is the grand immovable, unshakable, unburnable architecture of time.

Remember the seventh day when God rested; it was the time that was sanctified as holy, not the space. On Mount Sinai the time was special, not the place. For the Last Supper, it was the time that was special, not the place.

The only way to master time is a complete release from the deafening consumerism of the day and a release from being yoked to toil. Sabbath was never supposed to be legalistic, but rather an experienced reminder of joy, a disciplined reminder of eternity grounded in time, not space. Sabbath was instituted so that we might experience rest, edification, and sanctification. Our worship song doesn't have a space; it sits in time. We remaster time on a day of rest (sabbath) by learning that time holds tranquillity, serenity, peace, and repose. Stillness, peace, and repose become the heartbeat of a day in time constructed to master time.

Sometimes, we need a reminder that "it is done," "the battle has been won," and "death has been defeated." These pronouncements still ring true today as much as they did when Christ and Yahweh proclaimed them. If we are to truly be a church of time, then sabbath and prayer must come from the back of house to the front of house and sit front and center.

Prayer requires no space; neither does sabbath; they are the tools by which a church learns to master time. If we are to champion Jesus, then the church has to function as a stark contrast to society's obsession with space. We do not need it; it should not be our Master. We are a religion of time, and the profound thing that happens is when we master time with time, we conquer space and sanctify it as a byproduct of time.

Sabbath (*Shabbat*) comes with its own holiness; we enter not simply a day, but an atmosphere. It is an intrusion of peace, rest, and joy designed to sit counter to the noise of consumerism and toil. Free of striving and achieving, it is a chance to give thanks and rest and delight. If the church cultivated a spirit of rejuvenation that fostered a sabbath experience predicated on celebrating the goodness and blessing of God, we would champion a counter-cultural revolution.

Yes, your space is special but only because of the time you spend in it. The time dedicated to praise, prayer, and proclamation has sanctified the space. You could achieve the same results at a waste management facility with the same group of people. Time is the elusive perpetual commodity that we will never master, yet we have been taught to glorify time with time. Therefore, we conquer space for six days, but there is something special about the sanctification of the seventh day where we use time to make it holy.

I wonder if the next iteration of the church will focus on the crafting of times, not spaces. The best church I ever experienced was a time-construct in caves and cars, sharing moments together. "Creation is the language of God, Time is His Song, and things of space the consonants in the song. To sanctify time is to sing the vowels in unison with Him."[7]

Top Five Weirdest Church Moments

This list should probably be permanently in development. I regularly forget many of these weird moments. Then, on a night when I'm sipping whiskey with the boys, we unwind about some of the weird people at church. I share this only to say, leading a church can get very weird. We church this stuff up and pour grace on it and try to wrap it up in the transcendent love of Jesus.

1. **Flower lady's rule:** I was expected to call Daphne, the lady who did the floral arrangements each Sunday, before Wednesday, to let her know what the Sunday sermon was going to be on so she could pick appropriate flowers for decorating the church. I was berated by the senior pastor one time because I didn't call her early enough. She once berated me because I changed the message from Psalms to Romans because that shifted her entire bouquet motif.

According to her, Romans was roses, clear as day. I suggested that Romans Roses was utterly too predictable and some might say derivative. This was met with the wrath of a thousand fires and an explanation of my youthful foolishness, and a reminder that I should know my place.

Daphne was convinced that Psalms called for a peony-inspired affair that required a strong presence of white intermingled with yellow accents. The thought of Thursday transitions from this serene space to a more passionate red affair has caused quite a stir. Daphne, the flower lady, who is now buried under flowers at a local cemetery, was adamant that my lackadaisical approach to life was most likely going to end in a firing. It ended with a two-hour Monday meeting explaining the importance of all the gifts within our community and a willingness to work together.

Later that year I asked Daphne what I would have to preach on to get Venus Fly Trap and other carnivorous plants as a floral arrangement. She did not find the joke amusing. I suggested that Daniel might be the most appropriate biblical book to warrant a Venus Fly Trap arrangement. Without the intervention of Yahweh, there might be little or no hope for a person stuck in an impossible predicament.

2. **My first time shooting a gun was with Border Patrol:** OK . . . so they were off duty, but when I moved to Arizona, I had never fired a weapon before. When I shared that fact one Sunday, I was cornered after church by

three hulking Americans. They informed me that they would like to take me shooting after church and would pick me up later in the afternoon. Boy, was I excited! They told me that they would provide everything, and I just needed to be ready to go.

So, they arrived in a 1980s-style pickup, and we loaded up three-across on a bench seat and trundled out into the middle of the Arizona desert. Along the way, I asked, "Are you sure there is a shooting range here? This looks like nothing?" One of them calmly said, "Nothing is the best place to shoot."

We rounded a corner and stopped at a gentle little canyon that had clearly been used multiple times for shooting. We unloaded from the truck and headed to the pickup tray at the back. A rug was removed to reveal an arsenal of guns and some giant Disney princesses. I asked, "What is Snow White here for?" They said, "Tactical course."

They proceeded to set up the seven life-sized cut-out Disney princesses as a tactical course that we were going to shoot at: Snow White, Cinderella, Ariel, Mulan, Cinderella again, and Ursula. OK, the last one got tagged a lot and is clearly not a princess.

We shot 30 ought 30s, 44s, shotguns with tactical stocks, and ARs; it was totally incredible all afternoon, until I attempted to shoot a Saguaro cactus, which immediately caused everything to stop. My off-duty Border Patrol friends promptly told me that if I had hit the cactus, that would have been a felony offense. We quietly loaded up in the pickup three-across with me in the middle and drove back to civilization. I ruined one of the best afternoons ever because I almost became a cactus rustling felon.

3. **A RAV4 is not a full-sized SUV:** I did a mission trip from Arizona to Fiji once, which was frustrating because, it's way closer to get there from Australia. I took four middle-aged women to work on the opposite side of the main island, which involved driving from Nadi (the airport) across to Suva, and then inland to the rescue shelter.

Each of us arrived with two full-sized suitcases—a total of ten extra-large bags and five adult humans. We checked through security and were given the keys to a small early 2000s Toyota RAV4, which had four completely bald tires on it. It was monsoon rain season, and we had no roof racks. I spent the next eight hours driving across the nation of Fiji to the shelter north of Suva.

When we arrived, we discovered that Noah, the chef, had been cooking up a feast that featured a locally sourced goat curry and mixed seafood stew. We ate and immediately threw up before retiring to the room. I then drove to the local shops and bought a BBQ chicken and rolls, which we secretly consumed in our dorm rooms.

The missions pastor called me and asked how the trip was going. That was the first time I ever used an F-Bomb formally to another pastor in North America to describe how it was going. I said, "Mat, I've just had the most harrowing F-ed up day I could have ever possibly experienced—all while looking after four of my mums. Don't call me again." I never got asked to lead another mission trip, and I am really thankful for that.

4. **Pastors need editors:** There's a million examples of mix-ups when it comes to printing stuff. I worked for a church called Macquarie Chapel in Eastwood. We decided because we were near a university, we would do the opening day and hand out water bottles. So we had 2,000 custom water bottles labeled with an invitation to our church.

   The only problem was we didn't proof the text, so when the water bottles arrived, they said "Macquaire" Chapel, so for six hours on the university opening day, we were ruthlessly mocked by students over our terrible name. We handed out every single one of those stupid water bottles for free, and not a single soul showed up at church on Sunday.

   I would say as an exercise in building resilience, the six hours of constant mocking did really help to build up a tolerance for complaining. People love to complain at church. If you ever need a resilience-building exercise, fail to proofread something, make a mistake; then surround yourself with university students who will take delight in tearing shreds off church folks.

5. **I once asked a topless waitress to be a Bible study leader:** In the States, we lived close to a Casino that had a Burlesque-style bar as a promo on certain nights of the week featuring some fairly raunchy waitresses. At the same time, the global financial crisis was hitting, and

people were losing their homes. We were launching a church, and a bunch of people were coming to church.

The church was seeing a massive explosion, and one Sunday I asked a young woman if she would be willing to lead a women's Bible study. She explained that she was a brand-new Christian. I asked her how new she was. She said she had only been a believer for two months. I suggested the best time to start trying something is now. She then explained that she worked in the local burlesque bar as a waitress and knew that probably wasn't a good thing. She had applied for a transfer, but it wasn't official yet.

I suggested that she shouldn't hold the Bible study at work; she agreed. She was a great Bible study leader, and she eventually moved into management and then into another organization.

I wonder if there is a measure of real-time grace we are missing in the church. So many of the biblical characters have massive human flaws but we still love them; that's retroactive grace, and we're great with that. I'm just wondering in a moment of honesty whether the administration of real-time grace is the thing we struggle with the most.

Illegal Basketball Uniforms

For my breakfast radio show, I secretly created basketball uniforms for our breakfast team. I had them printed with the company logos and colors—all without the permission of the marketing department. I presented uniforms to the team live on air, and it was a rousing fun segment.

Right up until the marketing department found out about it. They were livid. Then the boss called us live on air and chastised me for doing this without consulting anyone. What had seemed like a good plan rapidly dissolved into a garbage fire. This made for awkward radio, but it was supposed to teach a point. Although we couldn't keep the most legendary basketball uniforms ever created, they were raffled off to raise money for charity. We wanted to establish with the show that it was possible to make a big mistake, upset some people, and then properly resolve the situation in a way we could move forward.

We wanted to create space on the breakfast show for people to honestly make mistakes and create margins where we could apologize, reconcile, and move forward. The thing about mistakes is sometimes you have to take the lead on them. My basketball uniform mess-up, which angered multiple departments, allowed us to dish out real-time grace.

The modern church struggles with grace in real time. Scripture is littered with examples of failing leadership—people we revere, who continue to lead after monumental failures. Israel had a whole era of useless kings. David killed one of his best soldiers and slept with his wife. Just run the list of Bible big names, and you'll see that there isn't a single one who didn't mess up some way. But they all continued to play a part in the church, and we don't seem to have a problem with that.

That's the marvel of retroactive grace. When we liberally apply retroactive grace to a historic biblical encounter, the warts of that individual can be covered over. In church, people regularly mess up in real time, so we should administer grace in real time.

People have big issues and make big mistakes—all requiring liberal measures of grace to overcome them. On radio I used to scream, "Swell apology music!" And I would issue a formal apology for a mistake; listeners would do the same when they needed to say sorry. We wanted to remove the stigma of messing up and just live in a messy show where accidents happen regularly, and there was a way to make up for it.

We bemoan modern leaders for their issues and mess-ups; we can figure out some robust reconciliation plan, but real-time grace is messy and awkward. Every church should have protections, accountability, and codes of conduct. They aren't going to be perfect though because church is messy, people are messy, and grace is administered real time.

And as 1 Peter 4:10 says, *"Each of you should use whatever gift you have received to serve others, as faithful stewards of God's grace in its various forms."* In our daily interactions, we're called to extend grace to others just as we have received it ourselves, embracing the messy and awkward moments with the assurance that grace is always available. Brennan Manning put it this way:

> Here is revelation bright as the evening star: Jesus comes for sinners, for those as outcast as tax collectors and for those caught up in squalid choices and failed dreams. He comes for corporate executives, street people, superstars, farmers, hookers, addicts, IRS agents, AIDS victims, and even used car salesmen. Jesus not only talks with these people but dines with them—fully aware that His table fellowship with sinners will raise the eyebrows of religious bureaucrats who hold up the robes and insignia of their authority to justify their condemnation of the truth and their rejection of the gospel of grace.[8]

When we frame up real-time grace, we live it with people who desperately need it. It becomes the revelation that we wear bright as the morning sun. This is not to say that we become perfect reflections of Jesus; no, we are broken vessels daily in need of redemption on the path to eternity, standing as beacons for all those with whom we break bread in fellowship.

Mark 10: 35–37 continues an encounter between James, John, and Jesus—one that shows a profound unawareness of what Jesus is being called to do alongside real-time grace:

> *Then James and John, the sons of Zebedee, came to him. "Teacher," they said, "we want you to do for us whatever we ask." "What do you want me to do for you?" he asked. They replied, "Let one of us sit at your right and the other at your left in your glory."*

Feels like my kid negotiating with me for a present leading up to Christmas. This request follows Jesus predicting His own death and explaining the course of events leading up to this moment. Jesus's response to them is firmly rooted in a place of love, together with truth.

> *"You don't know what you are asking," Jesus said. "Can you drink the cup I drink or be baptized with the baptism I am baptized with?" "We can," they answered. Jesus said to them, "You will drink the cup I drink and be baptized with the baptism I am baptized with, but to sit at my right or left is not for me to grant. These places belong to those for whom they have been prepared."*
> —Mark 10:38–40

James and John cannot walk the same path as Jesus; there can be only one Savior, and his name is Jesus. He does let them experience the suffering that that is to come and so walk in His footsteps, but Jesus recognizes that certain things are not for Him to give. While James and John have overstepped, Jesus quickly communicates what they can endure and the firm boundaries for what they cannot receive.

I think the most powerful expression of grace comes at the end of this passage. Our journey in leadership isn't a scramble toward the top, but rather a descent into humility. Our truest expression of grace mimics Jesus; it is found at the bottom of the room in service rather than the top of the room in the quest for earthly glory. Aware that the disciples are now frustrated, He calls them together to teach them this essential point:

> *When the ten heard about* [their request], *they became indignant with James and John. Jesus called them together and said, "You know that those who are regarded as rulers of the Gentiles lord it over them, and their high officials exercise authority over them. Not so with you. Instead, whoever wants to become great among you must be your servant, and whoever wants to be first must be slave of all. For even the Son of Man did not come to be served, but to serve, and to give his life as a ransom for many."*
> —Mark 10:41–45

Quests for perfection, to be right, and lead from the top are counterintuitive to Jesus's method and revelation. Our best lives are lived at the bottom, serving and empowering people in an upside leadership model serving up, not down, acknowledging failure and creating paths for restoration. Jesus doesn't berate James and John for their ludicrous request, but He allows them to participate in the journey, however painful and difficult that decision might be for them to endure.

Jesus's call to sacrifice, might be the most profound reflection of grace. As I shared earlier, ego led me to make illegal basketball uniforms unaware of the damage I was causing to the system. However, grace allowed that mistake to be turned into something remarkable—a teaching moment illustrating that community service starts at the bottom, not at the top. Jesus's lesson in Mark 11 is far greater; it is a life-or-death lesson, showing that greatness is measured in sacrifice and service. None is greater than what Jesus does for us.

Learning to Live by Grace

In the tapestry of Christian theology, grace weaves its threads in various hues, each version representing a unique facet of divine favor. I want to spend a moment walking through the various forms of His wondrous grace:

- **Saving Grace:** Like a radiant sunrise, saving grace illuminates the path to redemption, offering salvation as a gift from God. It is by this grace that believers are rescued from the darkness of sin and granted eternal life. Saving grace is like a torchlight of hope, illuminating the lowly road and pointing the way to salvation. It is not the first grace we encounter, but it is so powerful that it pushes us toward eternity.

  For it is by grace you have been saved, through faith—and this is not from yourselves, it is the gift of God—not by works, so that no one can boast.

  —Ephesians 2:8–9

- **Sustaining Grace:** Amid life's tempests, sustaining grace stands as an unwavering lighthouse, guiding believers through trials and tribulations. It provides strength and perseverance, ensuring that they never walk alone. When life's torment gathers its strongest assaults, there is sustaining grace to bring about a renewed strength. Our rock is Christ and His glorious strength. Sustaining grace is a force multiplier in conflict, pushing us past our limits because of a firm foundation.

But he said to me, "My grace is sufficient for you, for my power is made perfect in weakness." Therefore I will boast all the more gladly about my weaknesses, so that Christ's power may rest on me.
—2 Corinthians 12:9

- **Sanctifying Grace:** As a master sculptor molds clay, sanctifying grace shapes believers into vessels of holiness, transforming their hearts and minds to reflect the likeness of Christ. As a daily reminder that our transcendent God is also a local resident, we find sanctifying grace at work every day. The sketchbook and the journal keep account of these moments, and as we read back through them, we can see the works of God.

But grow in the grace and knowledge of our Lord and Savior Jesus Christ. To him be glory both now and forever! Amen.
—2 Peter 3:18

- **Prevenient Grace:** Like a gentle breeze preceding a storm, prevenient grace prepares the hearts of humanity, drawing them toward God's embrace and paving the way for reconciliation. More than a subtle irresistible force connected to the testimonies of creation, it is present and singing in chorus everywhere. Where a person's spirit is being gently stirred to eternity, there is the gentle, soft hum, building to a praise chorus.

  No one can come to me unless the Father who sent me draws them, and I will raise them up at the last day.
  —John 6:44

- **Common Grace:** Blanketing creation like a warm embrace, common grace bestows blessings upon all, regardless of faith or merit. It encompasses God's goodness, mercy, and provision for humanity. Common grace is on display everywhere for all people at all times. I wonder if this first grace is so good and so prevalent that we miss it regularly because the noise of distress overwhelms common grace's song.

  He causes his sun to rise on the evil and the good, and sends rain on the righteous and the unrighteous.
  —Matthew 5:45

Just as each stroke contributes to a masterpiece, these types of grace intertwine to form a tapestry of divine love and mercy, revealing the richness of God's character and the depth of His care for His creation.

No matter the corner of the artwork in Christian theology, there is a shared understanding of grace: the unmerited favor and divine assistance bestowed upon humanity by God. Whether it is the sovereign act of God at work in His predestined election or the cooperative play between God's grace and human response that sits within Arminian theology, the essence of grace is common. Salvation is a gift from God, initiated and sustained by God's grace alone.

The diversity of perspectives on grace should serve to enrich our experience by highlighting all the different strands at work in this glorious tapestry. Whether an individual chooses to express this grace through sacraments, the preaching of the Word, or acts of love and service, we can find intersections of grace in each facet of a believer's life. Theological debate on grace should serve to highlight the transcendent nature of God, the transformative power of grace, and the expression of God's unfailing love present in grace each day, encouraging believers to delve deeper into the fullest experience of God's present grace.

Church Planting 101

In 2008, my wife and I decided to move to Phoenix, Arizona. We were convinced we wanted to learn how to plant a church and saw an incredible opportunity in a community just outside Phoenix called Maricopa. I'm deeply grateful to Josh and Mat, the pastors there at the time, who took a chance on a twenty-eight-year-old pastor from Australia they had never met.

I've never been great at connecting the dots, and when we moved to the States, it was the middle of the global financial crisis. The US city that was hardest hit by the 2008 financial crisis was Detroit, where we lived; the city was severely affected by the housing crash. There were forty houses on our street, and thirty-eight of them were vacant. But in that season, our newly planted church exploded in growth. Hundreds of people were baptized, and we saw the Spirit move in powerful ways. The church was called the Church of Celebration, and that's exactly what we did for almost five years.

We later moved Phoenix to plant a church and minister there. For Halloween one year, we wanted to bring the community together, so we planned to hold an event in the parking lot of a Frye's grocery store. In typical church fashion, we called it Trick or Treat and lined up cars filled with candy. We prayerfully hoped for 500 people. That night, 2,000 people showed up.

The next year, we prepared for 4,000 people. We had 6,000. In our final year, we planned for 20,000. We booked Switchfoot, and nearly half the community came to a mile-long line of cars, and members handed out candy. It was the largest outreach I had ever been part of, and for hours, we shared Jesus with people, explaining why we'd put on an event like that.

Years later, at a much smaller church, we wanted to reach the community in a new way. So, we put on a stand-up comedy event. I had been developing a routine after my time in radio, hoping to become the Australian John Crist—or, more accurately, Nate Bargatze. I reached out to another comedian, Uncle Nath, who was already running similar events. Thankfully, Uncle Nath was further along the path and gave me insight into making our outreach event work.

Our little church hosted the event, hoping for twenty people to come. Nearly 100 showed up. About 70 percent of them had never been in a church before. We served drinks, did an hour-long set, and in the middle of it, Uncle Nath shared his testimony. A room full of people heard the gospel—while laughing and drinking wine. It was the perfect mix of Jesus, a little irreverence, and a lot of fun.

That night, some cultural stereotypes were broken, and people's expectations of church shifted. It's still one of my favorite evangelistic events—it was an easy invite: "Come along, have a laugh; it's only an hour, and you can have a beer . . . in church." The building isn't holy. The people are. And if you're about to draft an angry email, just remember—Yahweh gave the Israelites vineyards. They made wine.

We put on two very different events, but both designed to connect people with Jesus. Both required grace from those who had to navigate cultural discomfort in faith, trusting the process of reaching people who didn't know Christ.

Years later, a friend and I launched a podcast called *The Dead Elephants*. It was meant to bridge the gap between the pulpit and social media, creating space for healthy dialogue on taboo Christian topics. A local church invited us to do a live podcast as an outreach for their men's ministry. We partnered with three other churches to put on the event.

Before the event, the North American BBQ Pitmaster (yes, this was in Australia) offered me some home-brewed moonshine. I said yes. That might have been a mistake. But I looked around and saw how many people had brought friends to this fun, unexpected event. There was a level of cultural Christian mischief that felt . . . right. Sometimes, when Jesus isn't who we expect Him to be, He becomes exactly who He says He is.

If we create sterile, white-washed spaces that appear to be full of "holy people," we might be missing the point entirely. Jesus met and ate with tax collectors, prostitutes, and Gentiles. He wasn't afraid to be in messy spaces to communicate His love. But modern churches often sanitize events to the point that they're not relatable. Then we wonder why no one comes.

I once did a youth outreach, showing a Marvel movie, and the parents were furious. They said, "A church shouldn't show a mature-rated movie! Play something for kids." To which I replied, "To a room full of teenagers?!"

Ironically, many of those parents had already let their kids watch similar movies at home. There's a disconnect between what we allow in our personal lives and what we expect from a church. But church is where the sick come to be healed. None of us have it all together. One of the great joys of faith is sitting at the feet of Jesus, allowing Him to shape us into something better. So why aren't our outreach events fun? Why do we insist they be "safe" instead of engaging?

Jesus's first miracle was turning water into sixty gallons of wine. At no point did He follow up with Welch's grape juice to make a sobriety point. He ministered in the moment and used it as an opportunity to reveal who He was.

My point is this: Sometimes, outreach needs to be a little unexpected—a little disarming. A little *naughty*. It needs to prayerfully push boundaries, break assumptions, and remind people that Jesus is worth their attention. Teenagers don't want to watch *VeggieTales*. They need something real. But you might think, "Duncan, you're leading people into sin!" Nope. I'm just challenging us to be more like Jesus, who wasn't afraid to rub shoulders with sinners in settings that didn't look anything like a polished Sunday service. The sanctuary is often the last place people step into—so why not create invitational spaces *before* they get there?

Jesus is king 365 days a year. He doesn't take Halloween off. Instead of raging against culture, why not step into it and create something different? It just might spark a conversation that leads to Jesus.

Our Identity In Christ

In the beginning of the book of Ruth, we encounter a moment with Naomi when her life has truly hit rock-bottom. After losing her husband and her sons and being left destitute in a foreign country, she changes her name.

> *"Don't call me Naomi," she told them. "Call me Mara, because the Almighty has made my life very bitter. I went away full, but the Lord has brought me back empty. Why call me Naomi? The Lord has afflicted me; the Almighty has brought misfortune upon me."*
>
> —Ruth 1:20–21

She identifies as bitter. Based on her recent history and circumstance, we can understand why. The word *bitter* is a stark contrast from "pleasant," which is what the word *Naomi* means. Her recent history had led to a new identity, but there was a time when her parents had bestowed upon her a name that came from a place of love.

We can relate because each of us was first given a name that came from a place of love. There was a profound sense of joy in the moment when my parents chose to call me Duncan, which is funny because I'm white, and the name literally means brown warrior. I've never been in a war, so it seems equally hilarious that is what my name implies.

But my parents chose my name as a sign; hope, love, and joy were all present in that name. My birth name was written as a sign, a testimony, to who I might become. I had the same moment of joy when naming my children: my daughter, Ruby—more precious than jewels—and my son, Maximus, leader of the northern armies. Both names were chosen to represent who they might become; their names were given with love and affection.

Signs are everywhere, and each one points to historic moments in time, just like your name. A sign can be as simple as a name or as mundane as the sign that sits above the sink at church, which reads, "Your mother isn't here, please wash up after yourself." The sign on the community fridge says, "Please don't eat this food." Each sign points to a moment in history.

At some point, someone at church got so sick and tired of cleaning up the dishes in the sink, and that the sign went up—out of one-part frustration, one-part anger, and one-part good intentions. The notion in the beginning probably was, "I'm really over washing up everyone's dirty dishes. I want this kitchen to look good and ready for the next person to use it. I hope that our kitchen gets used regularly, but I don't want to be the only one doing dishes, so my hope is that each person will do their little bit to contribute." Sadly, that is too big for a sign.

A similar pattern likely led to the sign posted on the community fridge. We run a pantry and often have food in all our fridges to distribute first to people who suffering from food insecurity and second to anyone who needs some free food! Perhaps there was a moment when someone saw free food and took it for themselves, not realizing that it was being kept for someone who really needed it. If they had notified our pantry team of their need, our volunteers would have happily let them have the food, and prepared accordingly, but that didn't happen. So, our volunteers came in and were short-handed and got frustrated. So, they instituted a sign.

If you do this often enough, you can grind an entire community to a halt, with well-intentioned signs that signal that nobody can touch anything. They fracture the vision within a community and often speak only to the frustration of a history of events and not the deep desires of a community.

A dirty sink speaks to a busy church with souls hearing about Jesus. An empty fridge hopefully means fed people who don't need to worry about their next meal. Both these ideas are good, but the sign speaks only to frustration about a moment in history.

What Naomi is doing in the book of Ruth is no different. Based on recent history, there is no way she can be called pleasant. Her name is Bitter because that has been her recent experience. Have you ever had a moment when, because of recent events, you defined yourself as angry or frustrated. Perhaps those events have a longer history, and you now identify as anxious or depressed. Has history left you feeling unloved or shamed? In each instance, we take these names and start to wear them as our identity. Yet they are not who we are; Christ gives you names that aren't based on history, but on relationship. God calls you chosen, beloved, forgiven, and set free. God calls you a son or daughter. God calls you loved and redeemed by Jesus. These names are not based on a personal historic experience but on a current standing relationship. Right now, you are redeemed, loved, chosen, a son or daughter, and set free.

He takes those labels and places them over the ones that you affixed to yourself based on history. Where you are depressed, He places joy. Where you are anxious, He places peacemaker. Where you feel unloved, He places loved. Naomi begins to feel this transformation in Ruth 2 when she calls herself blessed.

If you are captivated by the guilt of your past, you will never be cultivated into your calling. Instead, you will sacrifice an alive future for a dead and buried past. God is sowing into your life right at this very moment; acknowledge that history doesn't define your future when the Good Lord is at work.

This is the praise chorus of Romans 8:39 where Paul says, *"Neither height nor depth, nor anything else in all creation, will be able to separate us from the love of God that is in Christ Jesus our Lord."* It's a right now love. That was present right when I wrote this line, and it is right now as you read it today.

In Christ, we are given new signs that tell of our identity in Christ:

I am saved (Romans 10:9–10)	I am an overcomer (1 John 5:4)
I am chosen (Ephesians 1:4)	I am powerful (John 1:12)
I am loved (1 John 4:19)	I am redeemed (Galatians 3:13)
I am free (Romans 6:18)	I am healed (1 Peter 2:24)
I am wonderfully made (Psalm 139:14)	I am transformed (Romans 12:2)

OUR IDENTITY IN CHRIST

I am forgiven (1 John 1:9)	I am victorious (1 Corinthians 15:57)
I am valuable (1 Corinthians 6:20)	I am salt and light (Matthew 5:13–14)
I am made alive (Ephesians 2:5)	I am strong in the Lord (Ephesians 6:10)
I am God's temple (1 Corinthians 6:19)	I am a citizen of heaven (Philippians 3:20)
I am a child of God (1 John 3:1)	I am never alone (Deuteronomy 31:8)
I am adopted (Romans 8:15)	I am reconciled (2 Corinthians 5:18)
I am righteous (2 Corinthians 5:21)	I am free from condemnation (Romans 8:1)
I am a saint (1 Corinthians 6:11)	I am treasured (Deuteronomy 7:6)
I am a masterpiece (Ephesians 2:10)	I am filled with the Holy Spirit (Romans 8:9)
I am an ambassador for Christ (2 Corinthians 5:20)	I am under grace (Romans 6:1-4)
I am justified (Romans 5:1)	I am equipped (2 Timothy 3:17)
I am God's workmanship (Ephesians 2:10)	I am sealed (Ephesians 1:13)
I am accepted (Ephesians 1:6)	I am called (Romans 8:28)
I am empowered (1 Corinthians 4:20)	I am born again (1 Peter 1:23)
I am blessed (Ephesians 1:3)	I am a fisher-of-men (Matthew 4:19)
I am more than a conqueror (Romans 8:37)	I am rescued (Psalm 34:22)
I am a new creation (2 Corinthians 5:17)	I am gifted (1 Peter 4:10)

Each of these attributes is predicated on a relationship established with Jesus that is empowered in your very life at this moment. They call us forward into a new future, built not on historic experiences but on a relationship that is renewed each day.

The next few sections might feel a little like a foundations course, but that is not my intent. What I want to do is to reframe our position before God to one that sits in a place of love and liberation from sin—one that feels measured with grace that calls us to something greater than ourselves. I'm going to touch on eight of these I am statements specifically about who we are in Christ.

I Am Chosen

I remember working for a large accounting firm here in Sydney when I was nineteen; at the time I had subcutaneous cystic acne, which was being treated with Roaccutane. I tried to avoid been seen, so I headed to work at six in the morning to avoid being on crowded trains, and I left work later in the evening. One day while I was at work, a manager came up and asked what was wrong with my face. The acne had been getting worse, and I explained the condition and how it was being treated. His response was, "This is why I can't book you for gigs with clients, because of how you look." That was a fairly brutal assessment, which probably could have been a major HR issue if I'd had the confidence to meet with someone about it.

This experience led to some serious depression for a couple of years; I almost completely dropped off the radar. I eventually dissolved any relationships that were going well because I felt like a total outcast. Recently, I tried to find photos of myself from that two-year span of life, and I could only find one photo. By the time the treatment was done, the acne had left scars on my face, and I had almost completely isolated myself from the possibility of feeling loved and connected to people.

Even today when I see a person with severe acne, my heart melts for them. I want to let them know I see them, that they are valued, and that they are deeply loved by their friends and family. That's probably because I wanted people to say that to me. Peeling back the scars of that season, I had a deep conviction that I would be the last person to be selected for anything—ever. For all time.

Two weeks after that incident at work, I was driving a group of people to university basketball tryouts. The whole experience was a train wreck; I was unaware of how badly Roaccutane had affected my ability to play sports. After two days of tryouts, I was driving back in tears after being told that I didn't make the cut for either team. What was worse, I was driving three passengers who had made the team. This only further perpetuated the lie that I was not ever going to be chosen for anything. Ever. For all time.

It's been a long time since those dark years when I lived through a self-imposed exile from people purely because of how I perceived myself. I was convinced that I was completely unlovable based on my outward appearance. The feeling of being an outsider and a misfit has motivated me to rally to the aid of anyone who feels like that poor nineteen-year-old.

It is important to acknowledge that despite my poor outlook, I was still involved in a lot of things and participating in plenty of social events, but how I thought about myself was based on how I looked; I always felt a little on the fringe of things. I was captivated by the lie that I was undeserving of favor or love—that I was predestined to being a side quest on the narrative of life.

Years later, I was sitting in a room with a bunch of pastors sharing that I didn't feel particularly well equipped to be a pastor. That's probably still true even as I am writing this. I felt like an imposter, as if I was pretending to be something that I had little competency in. We were praying for each other and speaking words of encouragement. Midway through, a pastor stopped me and said, "I reject the notion of you being an imposter." Like some kind of giant shot-blocking prayer warrior, he rejected my honest feelings and spoke a word of truth.

> *But you are a chosen people, a royal priesthood, a holy nation, God's special possession, that you may declare the praises of him who called you out of darkness into his wonderful light. Once you were not a people, but now you are the people of God; once you had not received mercy, but now you have received mercy.*
> —1 Peter 2:9–10

The thing that I was feeling wasn't a particularly true representation of what God saw me to be. I am not an imposter; rather, I am part of a chosen people, a royal priesthood, a holy nation, a people belonging to God that we might find hope in the truth that we are called out of darkness into wonderful light. There is no space or place for an imposter in that equation. Rather we are heirs to an empowered, emboldened faith in which, if we are aligned correctly, we will find ourselves in the truth.

So where is the alignment? Well, in verse 6 of 1 Peter 2, we get an explanation: *"See I lay a stone in Zion, a chosen and precious cornerstone, and the one who trusts in him will never be put to shame."* Jesus is the cornerstone.

If we align with Jesus, we find ourselves in this place of "chosen-ness." A cornerstone is the very first stone placed in construction, which is laid out to give a building direction. It must be placed true and level, and every subsequent stone finds its alignment based on that very first stone. If you are aligned to the cornerstone, then you are aligned correctly. If you are aligned correctly then you are a chosen people. Jesus said, *"You did not choose me, but I chose you and appointed you so that you might go and bear fruit—fruit that will last"* (John 15:16).

There is a purpose in God's choice, not yours. The chosenness is a God thing, but we play a part in the alignment to Jesus. When we find alignment, we find our direction and purpose. It is Jesus who chose you, so that through our alignment with Him, we might be able to bear fruit that will last. That fruit quite simply is the joy of Jesus.

I Am Beloved

I once visited a friend who had two children who were the same ages as our kids. When we arrived, they were quietly playing with Legos in the backroom. I consider myself a Lego aficionado, so I visited their workshop (bedroom) to behold the collection. They were engaged in free-building and were working from color-coded bins. When they finished, they gently packed everything away into the right bins, cleaned up, and went onto the next activity.

I was flabbergasted.

Someone once taught me there were two types of children, lambs and roosters. Lambs are gentle, sweet, and most likely introverted; they can dutifully play in the back room. Roosters, on the other hand, are loud and active. I want to suggest I have peacocks, who are even louder and more unruly.

My Lego room is a maelstrom of misplaced bricks and poorly stored systems. Scattered bricks lie throughout the house; my kids function like the polar opposite of what I was witnessing. I want order, but what I have is a furious collection of noisemaking individuals who honestly are just like me but with lower emotional intelligence. I fear for my wife . . . who is the only lamb in the bunch.

Often, I'll retreat from the noise; go on bushwalks; or listen to loud, chill hop loud, which only really adds calming music over the top of overwhelming noise. The reason I bring all this up is because I often wonder about expressing love. In our household, it's a deafening hum of noise, but love is still present. In my buddy's house, it's a quiet monastic experience, but love is still present.

How does Jesus express love? What is the volume at which He speaks love over our lives, and are we able to hear it? Or does Jesus's proclamation of love get lost in the daily activities of life?

> *How great is the love the Father has lavished on us, that we should be called children of God! And that is what we are! The reason the world does not know us is that it did not know him. Dear friends, now we are children of God, and what we will be has not yet been made known. But we know that when he appears, we shall be like him, for we shall see him as he is. Everyone who has this hope in him purifies himself, just as he is pure.*
>
> —1 John 3:1–3

There is a difference between loved and dearly beloved. There is plenty of stuff that I love; building that list is easy. I liberally apply love to a variety of things, including basketball, Brazilian jiu jitsu, Brazilian BBQ, donuts, and chocolate. Building such a list of things that I love is simple. I live in a big noisy house, and we often declare at the top of our lungs the things we love. We can get a big wild unruly list on things we love, and amongst our family we aren't afraid to share that.

Conversely, beloved is special, smaller, and quieter. The number of things that are beloved is a much shorter list. These are the things in life that we dearly love. For sure I dearly love my wife, Carly. I dearly love my children, Ruby and Max. I dearly love my flamed maple, dual-input Schecter guitar. The list of beloved things isn't big. This is a Christian book, so Jesus should be front and center on this list. Dearly beloved is a special position—the one that Jesus holds for us. When we use the term *beloved*, it suggests a gentle intimacy; there is a special place for the term *Beloved*.

But loving people is complex, isn't it? Loving people is complicated. It can hurt. It is messy. Because of this, we tend to insulate ourselves from the very people who need our love. The letter 1 John calls us to push past the fear of making mistakes or getting hurt. It calls us—Jesus's followers, God's children, and the Spirit's vessels—to love others. Yet again we see in this passage that God's chosen-ness is directional—from God to Jesus, so is His "belovedness."

The imperative calls for direct attention and reflection upon the amazing love God has bestowed upon his children. We are God's dearly beloved children, and that warrants an exclamation mark! There is a big ole exclamation mark upon our hearts that the good Lord place there when it comes to talking about His love for us. It is a dearly beloved exclamation mark that speaks to the depth, height, and width of Jesus's love for us.

God's love is foreign to humankind in that we cannot understand the magnitude of such love. It astonishes, amazes, and creates wonder within those who properly reflect upon it. Romans 8 screams this love: "Neither heights nor depth, nor anything in all of creation can separate us from the love we have in Christ Jesus!"

I think there is a real sense that being beloved and experiencing belovedness from God are two different things. It is one thing to have an awareness that we are beloved, but perhaps you don't feel it. So where is the path to experiencing that love that we so desperately need to hear? You are beloved . . . by the nature of what Jesus did.

John 3:16 is an imperative **For God Soooooooooo loved** the world. I might have added the extra letters for emphasis, but it is the same kind of imperative force that John is trying to communicate. We're not just loved, but we're so loved. What Jesus has done stands as the testament for his profound feelings toward you and me.

But we may be struggling to experience that love. It can feel a little like an arm's length experience. So, what is the thing that draws God to this love? Is it our loveliness or God's desire to see us seek our highest Good?

At our little church in Sydney, we pivoted a couple of years ago away from Bible studies and discipleship toward spiritual formation. The goal was to bring our people into a deeper awareness of the love that God has for us, which isn't predicated on doing things for Jesus but on learning to be with Jesus. This led to a whole bunch of confusion about what we were doing. It felt a little like a Harry Potter Wizarding experience of Jesus. The truth was that I wanted our people to have a mystical experience of Jesus—not from Hogwarts, but an authentic encounter with Jesus rooted in Scripture and prayer. I didn't want a program, but rather a prayerful and surrendered encounter with a loving God who passionately cares for us. If prayer is dialogue, then surely, we must learn to listen! If God speaks, then it probably requires us to be silent so we can hear. If God rejuvenates our soul, then we probably need to rest to experience the power of Christ.

This feels a little simplistic, but prayer seems to be the solution, but maybe not in the way you might be used to. Think about prayer in three forms. There is spiritual prayer, which is perhaps better known as praying in tongues or glossolalia. There is Kataphatic prayer, which involves praying with forms and images, the practice with which most protestants are skilled. Then there is Apophatic prayer, which is praying without forms or images, requiring us to listen rather than to speak.

Apophatic prayer comes from the Greek word meaning "without form or images" and focuses on the fact that God is both separate and different from His creation. Whereas in kataphatic prayer, God, through Jesus, enters creation as a human being and welcomes us into relationship with Him as one human being to another. In apophatic prayer, try to connect with the God who is not human; who is outside of creation and therefore beyond our understanding; the God who is mystery; the God who is pure love. So, whereas in kataphatic prayer, we mostly communicate with God through words, in apophatic prayer we put words to one side and attempt to communicate in silence with the God of love through love.

For us to learn to sit in the belovedness of God, we must learn to listen and empty ourselves of all other distractions. Our communication with Jesus becomes the silence in which we listen. We wait and we learn to be in the presence of God without expectations or demands.

I Am Forgiven

Each day we have between sixty and eighty thousand thoughts. Roughly 80 percent of those are negative. So, of those eighty thousand thoughts, about sixty-four thousand are negative. That is a boatload of negativity in your life; that's probably why when someone gives us criticism, we bottle it up inside and dwell on it for a week or two. Perhaps that's just me, not you.

On the radio show I did with my buddy, Sam, we had a text message line. Sam was often the fair and reasonable voice of the show, and I was more like a stampeding rhinoceros. We would often get texts from our listeners, mostly positive. However, a few texts were incredibly hostile—usually from regular listeners who would text the show to express their immense disdain for me. Thankfully, that didn't happen all the time, but when it did you had to be ready to move on quickly and not change the tone of the show because of someone's unhappy feelings about you.

I would photograph the text and use an Instagram filter to frame it with flames and play metal music. It made the text hilarious and for me, it completely disarmed the negativity associated with the message. I had to learn the art of forgiving quickly, so I could move on with the show.

When you are dealing with essentially a stadium full of people listening to each of your segments in a show for three hours a day every week, it only takes a small number of listeners to start the messages and texts flowing in. So, if you aren't good at forgiveness, it can weigh heavily on your soul. Their negativity is baggage that we were never supposed to bare. We have a God that loves us and teaches us what true forgiveness looks like.

> *He will not always accuse, nor will he harbor his anger forever; he does not treat us as our sins deserve or repay us according to our iniquities. For as high as the heavens are above the earth, so great is his love for those who fear him; as far as the east is from the west, so far has he removed our transgressions from us. As a father has compassion on his children, so the Lord has compassion on those who fear him.*
> —Psalm 103:9–13

Forgiveness is the release, on the part of the creditor or offended party, of any expectation that a debt will be repaid or that an offender will receive punishment for an offense. When describing the removal of an inappropriate offense in this way, the removal does not condone the behavior or suggest approval for the offense.

Forgiveness is the wiping out of an offense from memory; it can be affected only by the one affronted. Once eradicated, the offense no longer conditions the relationship between the offender and the one affronted, and harmony is restored between the two.

Forgiveness is ceasing to feel resentment for wrongs and offenses; pardon, involving restoration of broken relationships. Primarily, forgiveness is an act of God, releasing sinners from judgment and freeing them from the divine penalty of their sin.

Forgiveness is also a human act toward one's neighbor; it is given new incentive and emphasis in the New Testament because of God's forgiveness in the death of Christ. Hence forgiveness is a uniquely Christian doctrine.

> *We have been set free because of what Christ has done. Through his blood our sins are forgiven.*
> —Ephesians 1:7 NIrV

> *Therefore, there is now no condemnation for those who are in Christ Jesus, because through Christ Jesus the law of the Spirit who gives life has set you free from the law of sin and death.*
> —Romans 8:1–2

If there is no condemnation for those in Christ Jesus, we need to learn how to forgive others as well as ourselves. In his book *Learned Optimism*, Martin Seligman talks about the three Ps:

- **Personal.** We can feel like an attack is personally directed at us. We are the problem as opposed to the thing that was done to us is the problem. Often, we attribute a sense of personal attack when most often it isn't about us, but rather what was done to us. I might be broken and have an issue, but the world isn't out to get me personally. It might not be fair, but the world isn't biasing itself to humiliate me personally.

- **Pervasive.** Every part of me isn't affected by this. This issue that has happened to me hasn't happened at every level of society and isn't a cultural norm. We more than likely are dealing with something that is pervasively affecting all of culture. Everything isn't bad, more than likely this is a limited or one-off event.
- **Permanent.** Things aren't permanently broken, and nothing will ever be good again. In the moment it might feel like this, but that isn't truth. This event will pass, and we will find plenty of moments of joy and happiness, but right now in the moment this hurts. Things will eventually change.[9]

After an incident that upsets us, we tell ourselves that it will last forever, that it makes everything bad, and that it is all our fault. Being aware of these self-talk habits allows us to prevent them from continuing to happen. Things are not all your fault; the world isn't completely bad, and the situation isn't going to last forever. In light of Jesus, things can't last forever; Romans 8:28 reminds us that God works all things toward His good. And we know that there is no condemnation in Christ.

If you don't believe that Christ has completely forgiven you, then you will always try to perform to win His affection. Christ loved you in your sin, and you were forgiven from a place that could never have been predicated on your own actions. He literally models a profound forgiveness as a benchmark for us to live into.

Christ's forgiveness is transformative, not performative. The point is Christ calls you out of death into life. There is no workout routine to bring a person from death into life. That is a miracle of transformation that only Christ can give you, making you pure and new and holy by His own impartation of holiness. That is a transformation that only Christ can deliver.

Surely there must be something we can do! There isn't. People send angry texts for a million different reasons, and over the course of five years, I got most of them. There is no sense in me getting hung up and dwelling on them. I need to practice the liberating power of forgiveness, the very same liberation that Christ does for me.

You are forgiven—no ifs, no buts, no appendix with a hidden requirement. You are in Christ Jesus, so you are a new creation. There has been transformation and that isn't you—that was totally Christ. Our response is faithfulness to the imparting works of Christ's holiness. It's the best we can do!

I Am Set Free

I grew up going to a pretty conservative church; they were passionate about Jesus and Scripture; they had a creed and a prayer for every day of the week. Then once a year, they'd mention the Holy Spirit. I got the sense that we didn't talk about Him much because He's the wild and unpredictable member of the trinity.

Then, in my first couple of years of ministry, a charismatic friend invited me to join them at a church because a guest speaker was coming. I was reluctant; I was a big fan of the Wallabies (an Australian rugby team), and they were playing that very same night. Perhaps in a moment of conviction, I chose the church service over the sporting event. The service was rather straightforward with songs, announcements, and prayer; then the floor was handed over to the guest speaker, a lady named Faylene Sparkes.

It's important for you to know that I didn't want to be there, so I was slow getting a seat. When I entered the room, my friend who was sitting in the very front row, stood up and waved me down. This was not my dream location with absolute unencumbered access to a room full of raging charismatics. As Faylene got up, I lowered my head, hoping that like a dinosaur, my lack of movement might mean she couldn't see me. She could.

As I was examining the carpet and sitting more still than a renaissance marble statue, I noticed Faylene's two soft loafers directly in front of me. I looked up, and she said, "I'd like to pray for this gentleman here." What followed was the most inspiring and edifying prayer that had ever been prayed over my life up until that moment. Her prayer awakened something inside me; it had predictions about the future and a boatload of encouragement. Not only that but at the end of the session, they handed me a CD with the prayer recorded so I could go away and listen to it some more.

I was floored. Not literally. But I thanked the person positioned to catch me if I was slain in the spirit and told them I had a great base, a gift from God. Internally, however, I was trying to rationalize what I was witnessing.

Perhaps there is a spiritual war, perhaps the Spirit of God is actively at work every day of our lives, and perhaps there were miraculous healings and prophetic words spoken today. *"It is for freedom that Christ has set us free. Stand firm, then, and do not let yourselves be burdened again by a yoke of slavery"* (Galatians 5:1).

Galatians is an interesting book; it appears that the Galatians didn't get a bunch right, which often happens when believers fall back into cultural norms or historic ways of doing things. Paul has to recalibrate the work of Jesus and the Holy Spirit in their lives. What follows the verse above is a long dialogue about the nature of circumcision and the law through the lens of living in the Spirit of God. Finally, Paul lands on the very struggle of spirit versus flesh:

> *But the fruit of the Spirit is love, joy, peace, patience, kindness, goodness, faithfulness, gentleness and self-control. Against such things there is no law. Those who belong to Christ Jesus have crucified the sinful nature with its passions and desires.*
> —Galatians 5:22–23

Paul is no stranger to the spiritual battle that believers face daily. It isn't just an internal war. Paul points out that there is an external war at hand, one that requires the unique indwelling of the Holy Spirit: *"For our struggle is not against flesh and blood, but against the rulers, against the authorities, against the powers of this dark world and against the spiritual forces of evil in the heavenly realms"* (Ephesians 6:12).

We know that Jesus teaches this notion as well. He regularly demonstrates His authority over evil spirits in Mark 1 and Luke

10, for example. There is no shortage of passages that speak of the spiritual war going on during Jesus's ministry. Christ is the great liberator who is seeking to set the captives free. His power is unmatched, and His offer is a liberation that is only found through faith in Christ. *"But if I cast out demons by the Spirit of God, then the kingdom of God has come upon you"* (Matthew 12:28 NKJV).

Don't miss the implication of the work of the Holy Spirit in your own life. The kingdom of God sits upon your very soul and is actively at work, even as you read these words. This is further underpinned in the apostolic teaching of Paul, particularly evident in Ephesians 6 and 2 Corinthians 10.

Our early church fathers alluded to conflict of spiritual forces of good and evil:

- In his letters, Ignatius of Antioch (c. AD 35–108) emphasized vigilance against the devil's schemes and encouraged steadfast faith and unity in the face of spiritual opposition. He wrote about the reality of spiritual warfare and the need for Christians to remain faithful and strong in their spiritual journey.
- Justin Martyr (c. AD 100–165) discussed the role of demons in leading people away from God and emphasized the power of Jesus's name in driving out demons. In his *First Apology*, he argued that pagan deities were actually demons deceiving humanity.
- Origen (c. AD 184–253) wrote extensively on spiritual warfare, viewing the Christian life as a continuous battle against sin and demonic forces. He emphasized prayer,

fasting, and the Word of God as essential tools for victory. In *Contra Celsum*, he refuted accusations against Christianity and explained the spiritual nature of Christian warfare.
- Early Christians viewed the world as a battleground between the forces of good and evil. This dualistic understanding shaped their approach to spiritual warfare. In 1 Peter 5:8–9, believers are warned to be sober and vigilant because *"the devil prowls around like a roaring lion looking for someone to devour."*

The death and resurrection of Jesus were seen as the definitive victory over Satan and his forces. Early Christians believed they shared in this victory through their faith and sacramental life. Colossians 2:15 says, *"And having disarmed the powers and authorities, he made a public spectacle of them, triumphing over them by the cross."*

What I am saying is that the early church took spiritual warfare very seriously, incorporating it into their theology, liturgy, and daily practice. They acknowledged the reality of evil forces but emphasized the power of Christ's victory and living a holy life. This was combined with a strong reliance on prayer, Scripture, and a community of believers.

What is abundantly clear as we approach a notion of spiritual warfare is that the safest place for us to be is nestled at the feet of Jesus. Our commitment to prayer, sacraments, Scripture, and meditation on the Word of God become our greatest tools. It is Jesus who is our great liberator and deliverer. In Him we find complete freedom.

Sitting at the very heart of victory is the power of prayer as our most powerful tool to find complete victory. When I moved to the States, I connected in with a very charismatic group of people, funnily enough they were called "Xtreme Prophetic Ministries." I guess they were so extreme they blew the letter *E* right out of their name.

One of the things I loved was their commitment to prayer. They invited me along for a prayer meeting. Up until then, I had been involved in a pretty great Presbyterian church, who faithfully believed God had done everything. So, prayer meetings were a tight half hour with chatting on either side. Our XP team was on a different level; we started praying at nine in the morning and at noon, someone said amen. No chatting, no order, no agenda—just ten people in a room praying nonstop. I was out of my league.

When we finally said amen, I was floored and convicted that if I wanted to see this Holy Spirit at work in my own life, then my prayer life needed to respond to that. I'm still not remotely close to that room full of prayer warriors, but I'm willing to be on that journey every day.

I Am Called

In Ephesians 4:1, Paul writes, *"I urge you to live a life worthy of the calling you have received."* This verse reminds us that our calling is not just a vague concept but a specific, divine invitation to embody the values and mission of God's kingdom. Each of us has a unique role to play, crafted by God's hands and purposed for His glory.

Through Jesus Christ, who died for sinners and was raised from death, God is creating something entirely new, not just a new life for individuals but for a new society. Paul sees an alienated humanity being reconciled, a fractured humanity being united, even a new humanity being created. It is a magnificent vision.

So, if that is the vision that Paul is calling people toward, the second part of this is understanding how we live into the "calling" that Jesus is calling us toward.

> *Be completely humble and gentle; be patient, bearing with one another in love. Make every effort to keep the unity of the Spirit through the bond of peace. There is one body and one Spirit, just as you were called to one hope when you were called; one Lord, one faith, one baptism; one God and Father of all, who is over all and through all and in all.*
>
> —Ephesians 4:2–6

People are being called to be humble, gentle, and patient, bearing with one another in love. It is a spiritual unity bonded by peace. God's calling is universal to everyone.

Similarly, 2 Timothy 1:9 emphasizes the divine nature of our calling: *"He has saved us and called us to a holy life—not because of anything we have done but because of his own purpose and grace."* Our calling is a testament to God's grace, an opportunity to participate in His grand design, regardless of our past or perceived shortcomings.

William Wilberforce was a British politician and a key leader in the movement to abolish the slave trade. In the late-eighteenth century, despite being a young and successful member of Parliament, Wilberforce experienced a profound spiritual conversion that changed the course of his life. He felt a strong conviction that his faith demanded action in the face of the grave injustices of his time.

Wilberforce faced immense opposition, yet he remained steadfast in his mission. His work, driven by his deep Christian beliefs, led to the passage of the Slave Trade Act of 1807, which abolished the slave trade in the British Empire. He continued his fight until his efforts culminated in the Slavery Abolition Act of 1833, which ended slavery throughout the British Empire, just days before his death.

Wilberforce's journey is a powerful example of living a life worthy of the calling received from God. He used his position, skills, and passion to fight for justice and freedom, embodying the essence of Ephesians 4:1. His unwavering commitment to his calling, despite the challenges, serves as a profound inspiration.

People often ask, "Who am I?" and "Why am I here?" These are two excellent questions, but one is very easy to answer and the second one probably takes a lifetime to work through. It also probably has an additional question attached to it.

- "Who am I?" A beloved, chosen, forgiven, set-free child of God bought and redeemed by Jesus. You have an eternal visa granting you access to a heavenly realm that was bought and paid for by the blood of Jesus. Redeemed and set free, your identity is found in Christ who has empowered you with the Holy Spirit. Answering that question is super easy because it's the same for every believer.

- "Why am I here?" The universality of what people are being called toward is a humble, gentle, patient, and bearing with one another in love. It is a spiritual unity bonded by peace. Perhaps the Westminster Catechism summarizes this best by saying that our reason for being here is to glorify God and enjoy Him forever. So in short, your life should sit as a living testimony to God and His goodness regardless of where you are and what you do. A slightly easier question to answer but also pretty much a stock standard response for most believers.

The problem is that we confuse these two critically important questions with the frequently asked question, "What should I do?" which relates more to trade or profession. This question is more about my skills and abilities and how I make money. This question is not an identity question. We can miss the point that we are a beloved child of God before we are a teacher, carpenter, doctor, janitor, or bus driver.

This is the lowest priority discovery compared to the who and the why. Unfortunately, this is the question that becomes our greatest obsession—What should I do? Not once in Scripture do we hear about Paul's tentmaking ability. Today, we can't see any of his works. There's no Middle Eastern parchment that confirms his profound tentmaking ability—no comments from happy customers about the shade, comfort, and quality of his work. Calling is about who you are, not what you do!

Paul was only ever aware of the significance of Christ and the magnitude of the job of declaring that to everyone, everywhere, always. The size of your assignment never impacts the significance of your impact. One of the most toxic things that happened to us is social media; it is a constant buffet of examples of why your life is mediocre and everyone else is living on cloud nine. It's a caustic nightmare of lies that has empirically made people more depressed and anxious. Kids dream of being influencers yet feel the weight of failure every time they log into social media. It is crippling self-esteem and making us lazy, as we voyeuristically "perv" on other people.

OK, that might be a bit harsh, but social media is fundamentally affecting the way we engage with life, and it isn't healthy. Even Pope Francis is aware of the adverse effects; he observed that "another peril on social media networks is 'a false sense of belonging, especially among young people, that can lead to isolation and loneliness.'"[10]

So let me say this, doom-scrolling isn't the answer to what you should do. It doesn't shape identity positively. Remember that your eyes are windows to your soul; what we see with them shapes what happens inside. My recommendation is to consume about 99 percent less social media and replace it with . . . um . . . well, something that points you to Jesus. Colossians 3:17 essentially says, "Whatever you do?! Do it for God!"

I Am Serving

At some point in our history, many churches have substituted a transformative encounter with Jesus for a performance-driven ministry where our metrics for maturity are attendance and involvement in church-related activities. I don't think that should have ever been the metric for maturity. When I first penned this chapter, I wanted to make the argument that serving and reproduction are a better measure. But again, I think that might be inadequate. Reproduction didn't sit right with me, but I think it's a much more helpful measure than attendance and activity. If a person gets the gospel, they will share the Good News of Jesus and make every effort to share and lead others to Christ.

So, I'll just dwell on the first part, because I wonder whether deep spiritual formation might be the second part that sits alongside serving. "For the whole law can be summed up in this one command: *'Love your neighbor as yourself.'* But if you are always biting and devouring one another, watch out! Beware of destroying one another" (Galatians 5:13 NLT).

All over Scripture, we are told to serve the Lord. Psalm 100:2 says to *"serve the Lord with gladness."* Deuteronomy 10:12 says, *"Serve the Lord your God with all your heart and with all your soul."* Joshua 24:15 says, *"As for me and my house, we will serve the Lord."* And Paul in Romans 12:11 also tells us to *"serve the Lord"* (NLT). But then, in Mark 10:45, Jesus says, *"The Son of Man came not to be served but to serve"* (NLT).

Christians are free because they have been called by God—affirmed and loved and elected by God. We are also in the service of Christ. What we see in the notion of being called to "service" isn't a decent into legalism, nor is it an excuse not to change at all because of God's profound grace.

The opposite of fleshly living is love. The opposite of flesh is love . . . love that looks away from the self and its wishes, even its real needs, and looks to the neighbor and spends its resources on his needs. Christian freedom is freedom to love and therefore freedom to serve.

We are called to an imperative, to live the love of Jesus. First John and the books of Galatians and Mark speak to the notion of Jesus's service is prompted from a place of love for his people. Our bold response is to echo that love to humanity as a praise chorus for everything we do.

At the church where I serve, it is no casual coincidence that we are, "Living the Love of Jesus from Here to the Horizon." We have this on signs all over the place. I like things that say what we stand for, not against. My goal is to cultivate the most loving and Jesus-centered community I possibly can—people who are actively serving out of love, not out of legalism.

Yes, I'm orchestrating a rebellion that says there is a better way to live, and it's found in the teaching of Jesus. My serving is prompted by love, the love that Christ Jesus showed me first.

Thus, freedom and slavery are not simply mutually exclusive terms; they stand in the closest possible relationship to one another and can only be adequately defined in terms of object and goal: what we are slave *to* and what we are free *for*. If we are slaves to Christ, we can find freedom to live for his love.

You are in a perpetual state of being formed by external stimuli and the desires of our own hearts. Learning to be aware of this and to ask what we are slaves to and what we are free for becomes a beacon for our direction. I am a slave to Christ, and I have been liberated from sin to live in his love. Christ seems like a good thing to be a slave to—like way better than social media.

Let me tee off on social media and digital networks for a second. Research by Kuss and Griffiths found a significant relationship between internet addiction and psychological distress, including symptoms of anxiety, depression, and social isolation.[11] Additionally, a study by Lam and Peng identified a bidirectional relationship between internet addiction and poor mental health, indicating a potential vicious cycle.[12]

Social media addiction has been strongly linked to increased levels of anxiety and depression among young people. A study by Vannucci et al. found that higher social media use was associated with increased anxiety symptoms and depressive symptoms among adolescents. The constant need to check updates, notifications, and maintain online personas can contribute to stress and feelings of inadequacy.[13]

Another study by Leung reported that internet addiction had a detrimental impact on students' academic engagement and achievement.[14] In *A Non-Anxious Presence*, Mark Sayers also highlights the issue with digital networks for the church, as we become flooded with these anxiety-inducing systems. He makes this point:

> Any goals or programs of an institution that becomes overtaken by chronic anxiety will be replaced by the task of keeping the most dysfunctional members happy. Friedman saw this dynamic as cultlike. In this scenario, appeals to unity and inclusivity are masquerades to resist growth and any attempts at emotional renewal. Eventually, the herd instinct, rooted in emotional toxicity, will lead to fragmentation and falling out, as dysfunctional members of the system turn on each other.[15]

This is one of the reasons that our church (and many others) has made a conscious decision to invest in things that form us.

If the eyes are a window to our soul, then what we feed them becomes very important. We are being formed every day, and the question to ask is by what? John Mark Comer makes this point:

> For those of us who desire to follow Jesus, here is the reality we must turn and face: If we're not being intentionally formed by Jesus himself, then it's highly likely we are being unintentionally formed by someone or something else.[16]

If we are at the feet of Jesus serving him, it becomes easier to be formed by him. Our shorter attention spans, chronic anxiety, and increased depression are being empirically linked to addictions associated with digital networks. Where we hoped to be more connected, we've become more depressed and anxious.

I Am Reconciling

I was reading over my old talks in the hopes of ripping one off for this chapter, knowing full well I've done a bunch of talks on reconciliation. Typically, I have stressed that because Jesus has reconciled us, we are called to "reconcile" with our neighbors rather than push into a cultural phenomenon of honor and shame.

But in this chapter, I want to focus on the primary function of reconciliation:

> *All this is from God, who reconciled us to himself through Christ and gave us the ministry of reconciliation: that God was reconciling the world to himself in Christ, not counting men's*

> *sins against them. And he has committed to us the message of reconciliation. We are therefore Christ's ambassadors, as though God were making his appeal through us.*
>
> —2 Corinthians 5:18–19

Obviously, Jesus sits for a prototype of what we are supposed to do to the world. But how angry do we get when things don't go our way? I think more and more today, there is a simmering rage that sits just below the surface of life. We are at the point of combustion and looking for an excuse to explode.

This isn't how Jesus operates, and this shouldn't be how we operate. Jesus reconciles the world (and us) to God; we are called to be the ambassadors of this good news to the world. Our ministry is one of reconciliation through the lens of discipleship and evangelism.

So let me give you a brief overview of what an ambassador does. First, an ambassador is an accredited diplomat sent by a state as its official representative in a foreign country. An ambassador represents their home country. If we are pilgrims here, we must represent our home, which is with Christ:

- We build relationships.
- We promote trade and investments with Christ.
- We protect fellow pilgrims.
- We gather information on social policy and economic developments with the hope of figuring out all the intersections of the gospel and how Jesus restores those issues.
- We share Christlike cultural practices.

All this entails learning to navigate the language of our culture to communicate the truth of Jesus. We have a unique opportunity to find intersections between Jesus and life. Sometimes, we make this complex by introducing ideas like contextualization, but it's simpler than that.

Ever met a person who loves their Thermomix food processor? Or someone who is really into CrossFit? Or perhaps someone like me who is passionate about Brazilian Jiu Jitsu (BJJ)? It's amazing how often we can find ways to talk about the thing we are passionate about. It's the same notion as an ambassador for Christ, just without the sweet kimono and belt. We passionately communicate the things that have been significant in changing our lives for the better. But that's not all ambassadors do though.

Ambassadors are skilled in crisis management. An ambassador will assess and identify potential crises and maintain open communications, which means that we have a duty to be skilled in bringing about healing and restoration in challenging circumstances. Without harping on the ambassador analogy too far, I'll just say that our ability to adeptly interact with culture as Christ's representatives should faithfully portray Jesus's story and proclaim and invite people to participate in that narrative. Jesus has created an open door-open borders policy that allows any sojourner the right to have full citizenship and adoption into an eternal salvation through Him.

The thing about reconciliation that is often the hardest aspect to grapple with is sacrifice. Jesus's sacrifice at the cross brings about reconciliation, and it is this gracious gift that restores relationship. Sacrifice is the essential part of reconciliation that requires us to understand that it often isn't fair. On some level, we must grapple with what has been lost, be willing to accept that it is not coming back, and establish a preferred tomorrow that ensures the event doesn't happen again. Often, this will mean loss, sometimes heartache, and definitely sacrifice.

Matthew 5:9 reminds us that Jesus Christ made peace by reconciling us to God through his sacrifice. He is our peace. We are called to live in the very same way as Jesus. Corrie ten Boom comes to mind as an example of someone who made a great sacrifice for the sake of reconciliation. After the World War II, Corrie spoke often about forgiveness and reconciliation. She encountered a former Nazi guard from Ravensbrück, the concentration camp where she had been held. He approached her, not recognizing her, and asked for her forgiveness. In that moment, she struggled, but she prayed, asking Jesus to help her forgive. As she extended her hand, she felt God's love flood through her, and she was able to genuinely forgive him.

Corrie lost her sister Betsie in that concentration camp. That wasn't fair; it isn't just, and there is no way for her ever to get fair justice. Yet she chose the Jesus way and extended, at great personal cost, the same ministry of reconciliation as Jesus. We can also point to Dietrich Bonhoeffer's tireless work in prison or countless others who chose to push into the reconciling works of Jesus.

We haven't just been reconciled; we are constantly in the process and state of reconciling others to this wonderful work of Jesus. We should be more passionate than a CrossFitter, more enamored than a Thermomix owner, and more convicting than a BJJ practitioner.

I Am Loving

We decided a few years back to change the vision statement for our church to better encapsulate the essential underlying motivation of grace, which is love. So based on 1 John 4, we said the vision statement for our church is, "To live the love of Jesus from here to the horizon." Our goal is to be empowered as a community to go out of our way to share Jesus with the world, predicated on a powerful move of love.

> *God is love. Whoever lives in love lives in God, and God in him. This is how love is made complete among us so that we will have confidence on the day of judgment: In this world we are like Jesus. There is no fear in love. But perfect love drives out fear, because fear has to do with punishment. The one who fears is not made perfect in love.*
> —1 John 4:16–18

You might get lost thinking grace is some esoteric concept that is difficult to put into practice, so practice love. Straight from the mouth of Jesus, we get this*: "This is my command: Love each other"* (John 15:17).

Loving well has to start with a velocity shift. We must recalibrate our hearts to the speed of Jesus, so we can move lovingly like Jesus did in an unhurried, gentle speed where God can speak. In *The Ruthless Elimination of Hurry*, John Mark Comer makes this point about hurry:

> Corrie Ten Boom once said that if the devil can't make you sin, he'll make you busy. There's truth

in that. Both sin and busyness have the exact same effect—they cut off your connection to God, to other people, and even to your own soul.[17]

A change in life's velocity allows synchronization with Jesus. John 15:17 quoted above comes right at the end of the passage about abiding in the trellis of Jesus. None of that is rushed; it takes roughly three to four years for a grapevine to make fruit suitable for winemaking. When you tend to a grapevine well, they can produce grapes for centuries. The Zametovka vine in Maribor, Slovenia, has been around since the seventeenth century and is still producing thirty-five to fifty-five kilograms (77 to 121 pounds) of grapes every year.

Love is a patient pursuit and must be done free of hurry. It requires presence and time, and when we are short of those things, it can seem like the hardest thing in the world. Jesus's walk with His disciples is a slow walk of love, purposely moving at a speed where His beautiful creation can learn, make mistakes and grow. Love becomes a true north guide to every believer and every decision that we make from this moment into eternity.

> *Jesus replied: "'Love the Lord your God with all your heart and with all your soul and with all your mind.' This is the first and greatest commandment. And the second is like it: 'Love your neighbor as yourself.' All the Law and the Prophets hang on these two commandments."*
>
> —Matthew 22:37–40

Love is our starting point in an exercise that immediately leads us beyond ourselves. A statement often attributed to Church Father, John Chrysostom, possibly as a short paraphrase of Homily 50.4 on the Gospel of Matthew: "If you cannot find Christ in the beggar at the church door, you will not find Him in the chalice." We can live it everywhere, but it starts at the doorway to the church. Actually, it starts sooner than that; Francois Fénelon said:

> We are to follow God's grace, and not to go before it. To the higher state of pure love we are to advance step by step; watching carefully God's inward and outward providence; and receiving increased grace by improving the grace we have, till the dawning light becomes the perfect day.[18]

Many of us struggle to just be in the presence of God because we are afraid of the revelation that might unfold. He deeply loves you, desires your close affection and more than any act you might do in His name, He is seeking your undivided attention.

After a Jiu Jitsu sparring session at the gym with a close friend, Liam, he told me that he loved the waves of the ocean. He explained that the ocean didn't care (he used the F-word, but this is a Christian book). Liam said that no matter what the situation was, you could find yourself in the ocean: The waves continue to be the waves with or without you. They are immensely powerful, something to be respected but also enjoyed. No matter how significant you are, in the grips of an angry wave, you are nothing but dust. No matter how angry you are, the waves of the ocean could take every last breath of rage and continue like nothing happened. No matter how much frustration you have, the ocean is the place where you can let that out, and the waves won't lose sleep. The waves are always there, and every time Liam visited the ocean, he left feeling refreshed.

Shouldn't we feel the same way about Jesus? Isn't Yahweh, the author of creation, more powerful than the waves of the ocean? Liam's point was powerful. We can stand on the edge of the ocean and marvel at the power of the seas, but it isn't the place to lay our worries and burdens down. The ocean does not care, but God does. I agree with Liam when I go to the beach, it is epic. Every time I get down to the ocean, I have a great time because it serves as an instant reminder of God and his goodness.

Once while my wife and I were living in the States, we became all too aware of how much we longed for the ocean. We were in Arizona, and the backyard pools at our friends' houses weren't helping. The local community pool wasn't good enough. We wanted waves and sand; we wanted to stare into a blue horizon and get lost (in our heads) in the ocean. So, we loaded up one weekend and drove six hours to San Diego to stare into the ocean.

When we arrived in San Diego, the cool ocean breeze reminded us of all the things that are good and right with the world. The ocean served as a giant testimonial to Jesus's love for us. We were exhausted . . . the ocean could take it. We were homesick . . . the ocean could take it. We longed for old friends . . . the ocean could take it.

After that brief weekend sojourn, we were energized for days. It was a circuit breaker that reminded us of Jesus's immense love for us. This is the catch though, similar to the ocean. Jesus does not compete with social media or streaming services. Jesus isn't in the business of screaming over your calendars and reminders. Jesus is always there, but He will not compete with lesser things to find your favor. You have to consciously go to Him. He is bigger than the ocean. God loves you.

Once you've recalibrated to experience the immense love of God, living that love out becomes possible, but you can also fall into a profound cultural drift of busy. Every time you need to recalibrate on the ocean of love, remind yourselves of Christ's deep affections so you can pour that into the world. In your life that might look like the ski fields of love, the Sonoran Desert of love, the wild Redwood Forest of love. I'm Australian, and God's good ocean becomes my reminder every time I make the decision to visit and slow down.

Seriously, love needs to be the underpinning for all of this, but I didn't write that book. It's called *Here to Love* by Chris Cipollone, and he spends the entirety of his book underpinning the idea. If *Full Phoenix Rising* speaks to you, you should probably read Cipollone's book as well when it is available. He is also my podcast cohost for the *Dead Elephants* podcast. Hopefully, this nets me some of his royalties . . . plug over.

From the bottom of my heart, I believe that we only learn to love most fully when we can stop and be in the presence of perfect love. That reminds me of this statement by Teresa of Avila: "The important thing is not to think much, but to love much; do, then, whatever most arouses you to love."[19]

Naked Jim

I once preached a message called Naked Jim. It was based on *The Passion of the Christ* directed by Mel Gibson several years ago. It was probably the most poorly received message I've ever preached. That reaction might have been predictable although at the time, I felt like most people were commenting on the brutality of the crucifixion. The crucifixion's brutality seemed to be the main point of *The Passion of the Christ*—the central thrust of what Mel Gibson was trying to capture. For me the most powerful moment of the movie came in the closing scene when Jim Caviezel stands naked at the door of the tomb getting ready to walk out. It gave me goosebumps.

In *Theology of Hope*, Jurgen Moltmann makes a case that Jesus's resurrection both marks the beginning of the end times and initiates a future state for the Kingdom of God in the present age. It's called inaugurated eschatology. It's this idea that the resurrection becomes a force to awaken hope that drives us as a church toward a new righteousness, freedom, and humanity in Christ as well as a new promise of the future to come. The resurrection is the most important moment in *The Passion of the Christ* because it defines the trajectory of our future.[20] The resurrection future-orients us to a new hope. It seemed to me that this moment was in fact the most significant moment in the entire film; people preached on death, but life, perhaps even to the fullest was the biggest take away. To be sure this was a monolithic beacon of hope plunged into the world.

Naked Jim matters. What he represents matters: "The resurrection is not an isolated supernatural oddity proving how powerful, if apparently arbitrary, God can be when he wants to. Nor is it at all a way of showing that there is indeed a heaven awaiting us after death. It is the decisive event demonstrating that God's kingdom really has been launched on earth as it is in heaven."[21]

Rethink everything. What if there was a real and present way to connect and touch eternity?! Jesus's resurrection not only becomes a monolith of hope, but it pushes us toward God's universal plan for redemption. Suddenly, we aren't just connected to the now, but there seems to be a path that pushes beyond this realm into eternity. Jesus at the door of the tomb, on the third day, opened the way! Make the Third Day the priority.

The transformative power that was at work on the third day is at work now. It is something that signals a universal redemptive work:

> The message of the resurrection is that this world matters; that the injustices and pains of this present world must now be addressed with the news that healing, justice, and love have won. . . . If Easter means Jesus Christ is only raised in a spiritual

sense—then it is only about me, and finding a new dimension in my personal spiritual life. But if Jesus Christ is truly risen from the dead, Christianity becomes good news for the whole world—news which warms our hearts precisely because it isn't just about warming hearts.[22]

This isn't a feel-good story, but a feel-life for the first time story—one that features dry bones rattling. One that features a true, powerful lavishing of healing, justice, and love. We aren't looking to enter into combat, but rather to champion this news in victory. Yes, we aren't trying to win, but rather Christ has won! Jesus rose from the dead, and now the gospel is a universal good news story for everyone.

Deep in my core, I'm a sports nerd who remembers when Bill Simmons created the idea of an Apex Mountain. It symbolizes the moment when an athlete had reached the absolute pinnacle of their abilities. When a super-star reaches the top of Apex Mountain, they are unrivaled. The resurrection is Apex Mountain Jesus. Kevin Vanhoozer makes the point that the resurrection is the act in which God reaffirms the creation of the world and humanity after humanity's epochal failure, making the resurrection the climax of the divine drama that rectifies our histories and our futures.[23] Kevin Vanhoozer highlights the drama, demonstrating the intersection of doctrine and drama; I'm a sport fan, so I love to lean into a sports analogy; this is Jesus, atop Apex Mountain. It's a beacon of hope, a universal story of redemption, good news for everyone—Jesus atop Apex Mountain. It's the absolute linchpin to Christianity.

There's no sense in which you could divorce the resurrection from Christianity—no notion that this story can sit as an addendum to the rest of the narrative of Christianity. This event is so important that one must include it on all accounts and at every junction as the central narrative of our faith. Gerald O'Collins puts it like this: "In a profound sense, Christianity without the resurrection is not simply Christianity without its final chapter. It is not Christianity at all."[24] You don't get Christ without the resurrection. *The Passion of the Christ* has no meaning at all without the final three seconds of the movie.

The entire two-hour and seven-minute movie doesn't make any point without the final three seconds. Without the final three seconds, the story is merely a tragedy—a story of injustice, brutality, and the death of a good man. It becomes a tale of woe. But with those final three seconds, the entire piece is transformed into something entirely different. We view justice through a different lens in light of what Jesus does; we see ethics through a different lens because of Jesus. In those final three seconds, notions of immortality are shattered, and a new eternal promise is laid down and extended to all of humanity.

So, make Naked Jim great again. Three profound seconds make a world of difference. The power of Jesus is fully on display right at the end of that movie. I probably still can't preach my naked Jim message because it devalues Jesus too much. Salacious statements derail significant eternal ramifications. My bigger question is how do you cut through the noise of the world to make a point as significant as this? Sometimes, you've got to get creative about communicating the truth of Jesus.

When Do Sinners Stop Sinning in the Company of Jesus?

This might sound like a bold question, but Jesus seemed to be in the business of making big, bold investments in people—regardless of their background. At one point, I used to phrase it differently: "When did Mary stop hooking?" But there is historical research suggesting that Mary Magdalene was unfairly labeled as a sex worker. In AD 591, Pope Gregory may have contributed to this misconception, but the evidence simply isn't there.

What we do know is that Jesus surrounded Himself with sinners. Based on Scripture, here's a not-so-comprehensive list of the kinds of people He kept company with:

1. Tax Collectors
   - Matthew (Levi) – A tax collector called to be a disciple (Matthew 9:9–13).

- Zacchaeus – A chief tax collector in Jericho who repented and repaid what he had stolen (Luke 19:1–10).
- Various Other Tax Collectors – Jesus dined with them, drawing criticism from the Pharisees (Matthew 9:10–11, Luke 5:29–30).

2. Prostitutes
   - The "Sinful Woman" Who Anointed Jesus – Likely a prostitute, but *not* Mary Magdalene (Luke 7:36–50).
   - Prostitutes in General – Jesus pointed out that, because of their faith, they entered the kingdom ahead of the religious elite (Matthew 21:31–32).

3. Adulterers
   - The Woman Caught in Adultery – Jesus saved her from stoning and told her to "go and sin no more" (John 8:1–11).

4. The Demon-Possessed
   - Mary Magdalene – Jesus cast seven demons out of her (Luke 8:2).
   - The Gerasene Demoniac – A man possessed by a legion of demons until Jesus healed him (Mark 5:1–20).
   - Other Demon-Possessed Individuals – Jesus healed many who had been rejected by society (e.g., Matthew 8:16).

5. The Unclean
   - Lepers – Considered ceremonially unclean, yet Jesus touched and healed them (Luke 17:11–19, Matthew 8:1–4).

- The Woman with the Issue of Blood – Deemed impure, yet Jesus healed her (Mark 5:25–34).
- The Paralyzed Man – Jesus not only healed him but forgave his sins (Mark 2:1–12).

6. Samaritans
   - The Woman at the Well – A Samaritan woman with multiple husbands, yet Jesus revealed His identity as the Messiah to her (John 4:1–26).

7. The Thief on the Cross
   - One of the criminals crucified alongside Jesus repented, and Jesus assured him of salvation (Luke 23:39–43).

8. The Roman Centurions (Enemy Occupiers)
   - The Centurion with the Sick Servant – A Gentile soldier whom Jesus praised for his faith (Matthew 8:5–13).
   - The Centurion at the Cross – Witnessed Jesus's death and acknowledged Him as the Son of God (Mark 15:39).

9. The Rich and the Greedy
   - The Rich Young Ruler – Though he ultimately walked away, Jesus engaged him in a conversation about salvation (Mark 10:17–27).
   - Joseph of Arimathea and Nicodemus – Wealthy religious leaders who became followers of Jesus (John 19:38–42).

10. The Pharisees and Religious Hypocrites
    - Nicodemus – A Pharisee who secretly sought Jesus and later defended Him (John 3:1–21; John 19:39).
    - Saul (Paul) – A persecutor of Christians who became one of the greatest apostles (Acts 9:1–19).

The Reality of Sin and Regeneration

I highlight all these examples because we often assume that when people encountered Jesus, they instantly stopped sinning. But that's not what Scripture suggests. While there were moments of miraculous transformation—healings, exorcisms, and acts of repentance, there was also an *ongoing* work of regeneration.

To assume that each of these individuals never sinned again would be to underestimate the long, patient work of the Holy Spirit. Even among Jesus's closest disciples, we see failure—falling asleep in Gethsemane, denying Jesus, doubting His resurrection.

So, when did the sinners in Jesus's presence stop sinning? They didn't. Jesus walked alongside them in their sin and shame, never losing sight of the incredible promises He made and the potential they carried. He embodied real-time grace—never excusing sin, but never diminishing the value of a person, either.

His approach was breathtaking. Jesus saw the full weight of human brokenness but also the full potential of regeneration. He required only a mustard seed of faith; yet in return, He offered His own righteousness. That's an insane deal—low bar for participation, high bar for transformation.

Don't be intimidated by the word *regeneration*—it simply refers to the supernatural work of the Holy Spirit, bringing a person from spiritual death to life. Titus 3:5 captures it beautifully: *"He saved us, not because of righteous things we had done, but because of his mercy. He saved us through the washing of rebirth and renewal by the Holy Spirit."*

Grace, Regeneration, and the Messiness of Church

Following Jesus is more than a one-time decision—it's a lifelong journey of grace and transformation. Faithfulness is our part. Holiness is God's part. And that's an uncomfortable process.

I once argued on my podcast that if Lady Gaga showed up at our church, she'd be on the worship team. Why? Because she's insanely talented. And if we're going to practice real-time grace, we don't bench people—we apprentice them.

Church is messier when we commit to walking with people as they grow. It's easier to demand perfection before participation. But Jesus didn't do that. He didn't establish a finishing school to mold His disciples into theological powerhouses before sending them out. Instead, He *walked with them*—teaching, correcting, forgiving, and empowering them *on the fly.*

Jesus lived on Reconciliation Island—a place where you roll up your sleeves and get your hands dirty. The work of grace is participatory. It means failing, learning, repenting, and growing. Look at David: After his disastrous choices, he pens a song of praise in 2 Samuel 22, calling the Lord his *"rock, fortress, and deliverer."* That's the voice of a man who understood grace.

Then, in 1 Kings 2:2–3, David gives this final charge to Solomon: *"Be strong, act like a man, and observe what the Lord your God requires: Walk in his ways and keep his decrees . . . so that you may prosper in all you do and wherever you go."*

After a lifetime of mistakes and redemption, David still concludes that walking in the ways of Yahweh is the best thing a person can do. If you want to be a great leader, or perhaps a great follower of Jesus—start at His feet. That's where sinners, saints, skeptics, and seekers alike find the grace that changes everything.

Where Do We Find Grace in Abundance?

A great place to start is 2 Corinthians 8, where we find the Macedonian church demonstrating grace in a way that challenges and inspires us. This passage is often used in messages about generosity, but at its core, it's also a passage about grace—a grace that begins with understanding God's grace and then overflows into six different expressions.

The Greek word for grace, *charis*, appears ten times in this passage, revealing six distinct ways grace is at work in the Macedonian church:

- Grace as unconditional kindness, lavishly displayed (8:9).
- Grace as privilege or favor—participating in the offering (8:4).
- Grace as an act—being charitable and generous (8:6).
- Grace in living—sharing, giving, and helping others (8:7).
- Grace as proof of goodwill—offering or charitable work (8:19).
- Grace as thanksgiving—expressed as an act of benevolence (8:16, 9:15).

This explosion of grace in the Macedonian church didn't come from their abundance—it came from God's provision. Without God's grace enabling them, their generosity and joy would have faltered.

Grace in the Midst of Trial

Second Corinthians 8 feels incredibly relevant in our current cultural moment. Consider these words from verse 2: *"In the midst of a very severe trial, their overflowing joy and their extreme poverty welled up in rich generosity."*

Think about what's happening in the world today: housing affordability crises, rising costs of living, interest rate hikes, economic uncertainty, political instability, and multiple active wars. Severe trials can produce two very different responses.

Our first response is to retreat into fear:

- We become more frugal, less gracious, and obsessed with money and security.
- We hold tightly to what we have, fearing loss.
- We build bigger walls to protect what's ours.

Jesus warns about this mindset in Luke 12:18–24:

> *Then he said, 'This is what I'll do. I will tear down my barns and build bigger ones, and there I will store my surplus grain. And I'll say to myself, "You have plenty of grain laid up for many years. Take life easy; eat, drink and be merry."' But God said to him, 'You fool! This very night your life will be demanded from you.*

Our second response is to embrace grace:

- The Macedonian church pushed into grace instead of retreating into fear.
- They discovered that overflowing joy and rich generosity are God's response to severe trials.
- Their understanding of God's grace empowered them to be generous—even in poverty.

Grace changes our response in difficult times. Joy is the tool that unlocks grace in trials.

First, They Gave Themselves to the Lord

One of the most striking verses in 2 Corinthians 8 is verse 5, which says, *"And they exceeded our expectations: They gave themselves first of all to the Lord, and then by the will of God also to us."* Before they gave financially, they gave themselves to God. Paul makes it clear: Grace starts with surrender. Without a deep understanding of God's grace, we will falter in seasons of trial. But when we place ourselves in God's hands, He transforms our fear into joyful generosity.

Joy + Severe Affliction + Poverty = Wealth

This is God's economy, and it doesn't make sense by the world's standards. But when we rely fully on Him, we see how grace abounds even in scarcity.

No Plan B: The Persecuted Church

I interviewed Adam Holland, CEO of Open Doors, who works with the persecuted church worldwide. He explained that for many believers, "There is no Plan B."

- In persecuted nations, Jesus is the only option—not just one of many.
- They don't rely on their own strength, resources, or strategies.
- Their wealth is found at the feet of Jesus.

The Macedonian church lived the same way. They had nothing—except Christ. And He was enough.

Generosity Begins with Devotion to Christ

Paul highlights an important truth in 2 Corinthians 8:8–9:

> *I am not commanding you, but I want to test the sincerity of your love by comparing it with the earnestness of others. For you know the grace of our Lord Jesus Christ, that though he was rich, yet for your sakes he became poor, so that you through his poverty might become rich.*

Notice Paul's approach:

- He doesn't command generosity.
- He doesn't use guilt or shame.
- Instead, he invites them into grace-filled generosity, rooted in their freedom in Christ.

The goal is not moral obligation—it's a response from a heart set free by the gospel and ignited by God's grace.

The Starting Blocks of Grace

Where we begin matters. The Macedonian church didn't start from wealth or privilege. They started poor, oppressed, and at the feet of Jesus. This echoes the Sermon on the Mount, where Jesus begins with the Beatitudes—a declaration that the poor in spirit, the meek, and the persecuted are truly blessed. Sometimes, the best place to land is flat on our faces at the feet of Jesus.

A Lesson from the Slums of Bacolod
A few years ago, I had the chance to broadcast in the Philippines with Compassion International. I remember walking into a slum in Bacolod—a community right on the coast. Every time a storm hit, the entire slum was destroyed, and families had to rebuild from nothing.

I stepped into a tiny hut, no bigger than a standard-sized living room. Inside were a rickety ceiling fan, four single beds, and a small wooden mantle on the wall. Atop that mantle was a Bible. I asked about it, and they simply said, "It's the most important thing in this room."

Despite their poverty, there was profound joy in that home. They had discovered a Macedonian-style grace—a grace that transforms trials into generosity, turns poverty into abundance, and leads people to live with overflowing joy.

Some Final Thoughts about Grace
So, where do we find grace in abundance?

- At the feet of Jesus.
- In surrender to Him.
- In a heart set free by the gospel.

Grace is not just about what we receive—it's about what we live out. When we truly understand God's grace, we can give freely, love deeply, and trust fully—even in the most severe trials.

The Macedonian church understood this. Do we?

The Problem with Church

Take a moment and think about the last time you truly felt connected at church. What was it that made you feel that way? I wonder if we've lost sight of the purpose of church because we're too obsessed with trying to "fix" it.

What if the assumption that we can fix the church is the problem? Instead of striving to improve it, perhaps we should acknowledge that Jesus alone has the power to redeem the church. The reality is that the church is—and always will be—broken. There isn't a single change, strategy, or new approach that will unlock some hidden formula for a perfect church. Whether we make it more contemplative, more relaxed, less structured, deeper, or broader, there will always be issues. That's because, at its core, the church is made up of broken people.

In a YouTube video interview, Tony Campolo cites Augustine who supposedly said, "The Church is a whore, but she is my mother."[25] That's a harsh statement, but it captures a deep truth: The church is flawed, yet it is still to be loved. As noted, Campolo's assessment draws from Augustine, who expressed a similar idea with more nuance:

> Let us honor the Catholic Church, our true Mother, the true Bride of her Husband, because she is the wife of so great a Lord. And what shall I say? How great is that Husband and of singular rank, that he discovered a prostitute and made her a virgin. Because she should not deny that she was a prostitute, lest she forget the mercy of her liberator. How can it be said that she was not a prostitute when she fornicated with demons and idols? Fornication was in the heart of everyone; a few have fornicated in the flesh, but everyone has fornicated in his heart. And He came and made her a virgin; he made the church a virgin.[26]

Both Augustine and Campolo point to the same truth: Jesus is transformative. A church is only changed when it is close to Him. Christ is the liberator, the purifier, the One who accomplishes the impossible. The church is not meant to be a performance; it is a place of radical, life-changing encounters with Jesus.

Jesus makes the unclean pure—His work alone. That might sound like strong language, but it's exactly what God says in the book of Hosea. Paul echoes this in Ephesians 5:25–27, where he describes how Christ's sacrificial love sanctifies the church and makes her pure. Without Jesus, transformation is impossible.

If a church is truly a place of transformation, then everyone in the room is a sinner who needs Jesus. One hundred percent of the people who walk through the church doors are broken and should be pointed as quickly as possible to Christ. We need real-time grace, not just retroactive forgiveness.

In my years in breakfast radio, I conducted nearly 1,000 interviews—many of them with well-known Christian figures. And I can tell you, they are no different from you or me. From the bottom of my heart, every single person you might idolize is just a regular person who needs Jesus. I've spoken to them, and none of them have a secret formula that put them on a platform. If we assume church is about performance, we move away from the foundational truth that Jesus is the one who transforms lives.

Moving Toward Transformation

A church built on performance can become a façade—more like whitewashed tombs than a genuine encounter with Jesus. The solution isn't another strategy or program; the solution is Jesus. So, what would it look like if we moved closer to Him and embraced real-time grace?

- **From Performance to Presence:** If we prioritize excellence at the cost of authenticity, worship can become a spectacle rather than an offering. Our focus should be on cultivating the presence of God, not the performance of God. Worship should be a response to Him, not a perfectly curated setlist. Preaching should point people to Jesus, not function as a TED Talk. We must create an environment where people feel safe to be real—questions, struggles, and all.

- **Repentance as the Norm, Not the Exception:** What if we embraced repentance rather than pretending that we have it all together? Sundays should be about testimonies of struggle and redemption, not just victories. Confession should be a natural part of our rhythm. The gospel is clear: We are saved by grace, not effort. Let's live that out.
- **Real Discipleship Endures Hardship:** Church isn't about filling seats; it's about making disciples. A healthy church fosters deep spiritual formation, equipping people to endure hardship and follow Jesus daily. We should pray deeply, walk in the Spirit, and disciple people beyond a Sunday service.
- **From Event Management to Family Dinners:** Think about a big family gathering—everyone knows each other's names and stories. There's space for real conversation, for laughter, for messy moments. That's what the church should be. When things get messy, we pivot, prioritizing people over programs.
- **Messy People Are Welcome:** A transformative church is a place where people belong before they believe. That means we embrace the mess. We acknowledge that we are not polished leaders, and we allow people to move at different paces in their journey toward Jesus.
- **Real-Time Grace, Not a One-Time Event:** Salvation is just the starting point. Grace is an ongoing process, not a one-time experience. We should walk in grace daily, trusting that the Spirit is constantly growing, refining, and shaping us into the image of Jesus.

- **Jesus Over Everything:** If our church is built on performance, we will drift toward legalism, comparison, and burnout. But if our church is built on Jesus, it will be marked by grace, transformation, and radical love. The best place for the broken and downtrodden should be the church—because that is where true healing is found.

The church is not a problem to be fixed. It is a broken, beautiful, grace-filled community that Jesus is redeeming. Let's stop trying to manufacture perfection and start leaning into the only One who can truly transform us.

Pastor of Disaster

I've been doing Jiu Jitsu for twenty years now; my journey started in 2004 when I was giving a youth talk on evangelism. I told the group that we should have friends who don't yet know Jesus. Then, mid-message, I paused. I realized my entire circle of friends was Christian. I couldn't name a single friend outside the church. Right then, I stopped, apologized, and sat down.

The next day, I signed up at a Jiu Jitsu gym. I figured Ultimate Fighting Championship (UFC) fans were probably the hardest people to share Jesus with. I was wrong. But twenty years later, I've learned a valuable lesson: We should all be on mission for Jesus.

Over the years, I've officiated weddings for people from the gym. Part of my requirement is that I do a faith-based ceremony. We go through a pre-marriage course centered on faith, read a Bible passage, and I pray for them on their wedding day. Some say no, but many have said yes.

Being part of this gym has meant walking with people through their best and worst moments. Sometimes, we even pray right there on the mats. And almost every week for the past twenty years, I've had a chance to share Jesus with someone. For a while, they called me "Pastor D," and I still sign off emails that way. Even at the gym, that's what people call me.

One time, a famous female UFC fighter visited our gym. The coaches introduced me by saying, "This is Pastor D. If you want to know about Jesus, he'd love to chat." I laughed, but it was true. Jesus is my favorite person, and I want everyone to know that.

The Problem with Church Mission

The issue with mission in the church is that we think the first step is inviting people to a Sunday service. Honestly, I think it's the last step. That's why I chose Jiu Jitsu. I wanted to learn to share my faith in the most uncomfortable setting possible. If I could do it in a room full of trained fighters, I figured I could do it anywhere.

Jiu Jitsu is the most important time of my week. I prioritize it because it's rewarding. The issue is—I enjoy it more than Sunday service. Jiu Jitsu feels like a battle among friends. The sparring is intense. People are trying to take your head off. But afterward, we celebrate together.

Church, on the other hand, sometimes feels like friends at war. We're supposed to love each other. We're supposed to bond over Jesus, but political infighting and church differences often create tension. Sunday can feel like a ceremony of faith with an undercurrent of conflict.

Prioritizing the Mission

People sometimes get frustrated when I choose a gym event over a church event. But here's my thinking: The people in church already have an eternal destination. I want to be present for those who don't.

I love our church. I love our mission. But Jiu Jitsu feels simpler and less political. As a black belt, I've earned respect. I even had a custom rash guard made with an ecclesiastical collar and stained-glass design. It says, * Pastor of Disaster. * I love it. If I wore it to church, I might get in trouble. But at the gym, it sparks great conversations.

Jesus Outside the Church Walls

If we measure success by Sunday attendance, we risk prioritizing performance over Christ at work in everyday life. Most of Jesus's ministry happened outside the temple. And now, the temple is us—we are where the Holy Spirit dwells. Wherever two or more gather, God is present. Many places don't have a formal service but still have believers gathered. That matters.

I share this because Jiu Jitsu is my mission field. It's where I can be salt and light. And you have places I can't go. Maybe it's salsa dancing (which I personally can't stand—don't tell my salsa friends). But I know believers who are powerfully at work in that community. The same goes for ballet, musicals, and every other passion or profession. Jesus is present in all of them.

Living as an Ambassador for Christ

Sometimes, I feel like a chameleon—adjusting to my surroundings, not to blend in but to represent Jesus well. I'm rougher at the gym than I am on Sunday. My goal is to avoid hypocrisy while being a faithful ambassador of Christ. I don't always get it right. But I'd rather be in the game, practicing, than sitting on the sidelines.

You probably work a regular job, surrounded by people who have little to no experience with church. They didn't go with Grandma on Sundays. Their view of faith is shaped by biased media and misconceptions. But here's the truth: You are the church. The Holy Spirit dwells in you. And you park that church in different places throughout the week. The secret? Live it. Share it. Proclaim it.

Maybe faith looks more like van life—small communities on mission, always moving. Sunday is like a caravan park. We all pull in, celebrate the week's wins and losses, and remind each other that Jesus is at the center of it all. Then, we hit the road again, carrying His light into the world.

Nomads of Hope

I had the good pleasure of joining a team of fellow pastors at a conference, which was pretty much my favorite conference of the year. In fact, it was the only conference I've attended in years. It was seriously good being in a room with coworkers leading various ministries all over New South Wales. The thing that kept stirring in my heart though was a word—perhaps for me, and perhaps for our small crew of Churches of Christ.

Throughout the conference, I sensed that there were many nomads coming in from a rough and tumultuous season—one of great challenge and difficulty:

> "Numbers are down" . . . check.
> "Church feels like it's in flux" . . . check.
> "I feel at the end of my tether" . . . check.

We drifted down to Stanwell Park Beach, many of us battered and bruised and in need of some healing. Lord Jesus, please bring me some healing in Stanwell Park! I felt it too.

If we made a list of things in our local churches with which we are frustrated, I wonder if we would see that many of the struggles we face are common across the movement. I feel it too. I took a moment to look up the meaning of *nomads*. Dictionary.com defines a nomad as "a member of a people or tribe that has no permanent abode but moves about from place to place, usually seasonally and often following a traditional route or circuit according to the state of the pasturage or food supply." I wonder if with all this movement, unrest, and profoundly anxious season, we have forgotten our home. Church has closed, and people have moved on, and this has led us to question the permanence of our place, which has led to a great tension.

> Where am I supposed to be?
> What am I supposed to do?
> Is God closing the doors to this church?

I sincerely believe that we were always nomads. The idea of being a sojourner in this world is not a new concept. Hebrews 11:13 calls us strangers and exiles on this earth. First Peter 2:11 refers to us as foreigners and exiles. Psalm 39:12 calls us passing guests or sojourners. You my friend are nomads; you have not reached the home that Jesus is preparing in advance.

Our treasure, that wonderful saving knowledge of Jesus, was put into a clay pot, which is a temporary structure (2 Corinthians 4:7). Both Peter (2 Peter 1:13) and Paul (2 Corinthians 5:4) allude to our present form as a tent, which is the ultimate nomadic accommodation. If we assume that the "gig" of pastoring is a permanent thing, then we might forget the bold intentions from which we should lead. What if this great moment, this blue hole that Jack Reese writes about is an inspiration to work from the tent, moving toward the pastures.[27] Nomads don't stay in one place, perhaps the church is too much of a refuge in which we hide out.

The lamp placed on a stand isn't the church on the corner; it's you going to the pasture to be salt, to be light. *"Let us not become weary in doing good, for at the proper time we will reap a harvest if we do not give up"* (Galatians 6:9). Sweet merciful Jesus, this has been my verse for two years; it moved from being a tearful cry for help, to being a battle cry to persevere. But it doesn't start in the church with a program. It starts in the pastures of your community beyond the walls of the building.

The harvest to reap was never in the church to begin with. I've had to reframe the notion of what we are trying to accomplish in our church. Our church is officially a replant at our community. I have been blessed with forty to fifty faithful believers and a facility to operate out of. If you offered that to any would-be church planter, they would be beyond excited at the opportunity that holds. But that isn't the solution.

All God-things seem to start with a rag-tag group of unlikely believers who faithfully walk in step with Jesus despite the unreasonable odds. More likely, despite insurmountable or impossible odds—something so far-fetched that the only impossible way for it to happen is God. Honestly, that's a pretty liberating thought. I've been inspired by this old tale, which is slightly adapted from the original, which was about an adult man:

> A young girl was walking along a beach upon which thousands of starfish had been washed up during a terrible storm. When she came to each starfish, she would pick it up and throw it back into the ocean. People watched her with amusement.
>
> She had been doing this for some time when a man approached her and said, "Little girl, why are you doing this? Look at this beach! You can't save all these starfish. You can't begin to make a difference!"
>
> The girl seemed crushed, suddenly deflated. But after a few moments, she bent down, picked up another starfish, and hurled it as far as she could into the ocean. Then she looked up at the man and replied, "Well, I made a difference for that one!"
>
> The old man looked at the girl inquisitively and thought about what she had done and said. Inspired, he joined the little girl in throwing starfish back into the sea. Soon others joined, and all the starfish were saved.[28]

This story by Loren Eiseley isn't a Christian parable; it was published in a book called *The Unexpected Universe*. Eiseley was a naturalist looking to renew hope in the world in the 1960s. Awkwardly though, he has captured the nature of salvation: It matters to that one person. That one person's life is radically transformed by an encounter with Jesus. When that happens in the presence of others, it gives them just enough motivation to do the same. And suddenly, we've got two people believing in the power of Jesus.

So, dare to believe again my nomad friend . . . that we might bring the goodness of Jesus to just one person in our community . . . that it might inspire someone else to believe they can do the same. It's almost like mustard-seed-sized faith, isn't it? Those starfish need some mustard-seed faith to move into the ocean so we can move those mountains. That's a cacophony of metaphors . . . OK . . . I just confused myself.

The rally point probably isn't the church anymore; it's the coffee shop, the mall, the pub, the club, the sporting club, F45 Training, or the mixed martial arts gym . . . but we're not the center anymore. Church is the last point of contact these days; venture out my nomad buddies and befriend the neighborhood. They need the peace of God more than ever. The hope of Jesus without the constraints of institutional religious hurdles. Real community, real connection, and real love. All these things we have the gifts and knowledge to share.

It all starts with one person. That may be the inspiration needed to give another person the courage to join in. Nomads don't stay in; we head out to love, to be gracious, and to live differently. Nomads tend to be listless on an ocean of restlessness.

Recognizing and Combatting Persistent Restlessness

Here I stand in a world where emotional apathy sets in, where restlessness and dissatisfaction mark our lives. Lethargy takes hold, and we shy away from meaningful tasks or commitments; we doom-scrolling endlessly to distract ourselves from what truly matters. We worry about dopamine addiction or ADHD, seeking distraction and novelty just to feel something.

A mist of persistent sadness and melancholy lingers over our lives; its root causes are unclear. Numbness becomes normal; disengagement, burnout, and deep cynicism replace meaning, purpose, and joy. Our vessels drift on the sea of restlessness in the fog of perpetual melancholy. And we don't care.

This isn't new. Monks wrote about this mindset as early as the third century. They characterized it as acedia, a state of spiritual or emotional apathy. It was described as a condition in which individuals failed to care, even for the dead. It was considered one of the most dangerous spiritual states because it eroded the ability to pray, work, or serve in community. While many know of the seven deadly sins, acedia was classified as one of the "eight deadly thoughts." It is characterized by:

- Inner restlessness and dissatisfaction
- Spiritual lethargy or apathy
- Avoidance of meaningful tasks or commitments
- A constant search for distraction or novelty
- A vague yet persistent sadness or melancholy, often without a clear cause

This has been called the "noonday sin" or "noonday demon." Pastors are particularly vulnerable; after pouring themselves into

Sunday service, they collapse in exhaustion, finding themselves closest to God one moment and on the brink of despair the next.

Evagrius Ponticus, who lived from AD 345 to 399 (by the way, what a fantastic name for a future baby!), wrote extensively about this spiritual malady:

> The demon of acedia, also called the noonday demon, is the most oppressive of all the demons. He attacks the monk about the fourth hour [10 a.m.] and besieges his soul until the eighth hour [2 p.m.]. First, it makes the sun appear to slow down or stop moving. . . . He instills in him a hatred for the place and his very life itself, his manual work, and the reading of scripture. He suggests that love has disappeared from among the brethren, and there is no one to console him.[29]

Acedia isn't mere laziness—it's a deep spiritual apathy that saps our will to care about our own spiritual life and relationships. It's a weariness so oppressive that it crushes motivation. Maybe this explains the popularity of books such as *Atomic Habits*, which reveals how one percent improvement helps move us from listlessness to purpose, one small step at a time.[30]

I became aware of acedia in my own life when I started practicing Sabbath. I changed my Friday prayers (my Sabbath day) to focus solely on celebrating the blessings in my life. I created a "joy map," intentionally looking at everything through the lens of thankfulness. Room darkening blinds? Celebrate that I could sleep longer. Breakfast? Another cause for celebration. No matter what the state of my family, they were a celebration.

Practicing this regularly, I began to see and feel real joy in the ways God was showing up.

Acedia is sneaky. It disguises itself as external forces—digital addiction, the manic pace of life, but it is also internal. Thankfully, we are not powerless against it. Victory is possible in Christ.

Gratitude and Simplicity

Friday is my gratitude day; it's also a day when I try to avoid spending. The goal? Make do with what's already in the house. There's plenty of blessing at home, and for one day, I refuse to buy anything. Consumerism can rest. I'll be fine with simplicity.

- Develop gratitude practices—journaling or intentional reflection—to rediscover joy in simple things.
- Limit distractions, technology, and entertainment consumption to restore spiritual balance.

Routine and Stability (The Virtue of Staying Put)

One of the easiest ways to fight acedia is through regular prayer. Monks used bells for this. We use phone reminders for everything else, so why not for prayer? Set reminders to pray, reflect, or do an evening examen can anchor us. Psalm 133 reminds us of the great joy in friendship, so on Sabbath, I prioritize gathering with people I love—God designed friendship for a reason.

- Commit to daily rhythms of prayer, mindfulness, or meditation.
- Seek stability through community and sustained relationships rather than chasing novelty.

Mindfulness and Presence

Have you ever chatted with Jesus while cooking? Have you ever prayed before an important business meeting? Taking these small moments in the mundane can ground us in the transformative peace of Christ:

- Practice attentiveness in ordinary tasks (e.g., cooking, gardening, doing manual labor) to cultivate peace and satisfaction.
- Embrace silence as a spiritual discipline, resisting the urge for constant distraction.

Service and Connection

Our church runs a food pantry. It's also the place where our volunteers feel most blessed. In Australia, one-third of supermarket food is thrown away. Thankfully, there are ways to reclaim food that is no longer salable but still good to eat. We package it into boxes and give it to those in need. In the food pantry, our volunteers share life, struggles, and joy. In acts of generosity, there is little room for acedia:

- Engage in community or charity work to counteract isolation.
- Share struggles openly with trusted friends or spiritual companions for mutual encouragement.

Even Jesus saw this struggle in His disciples. In the garden, as He prayed, they fell into a malaise of sleep. Acedia is real, but it is not insurmountable. Small, intentional choices each day lead to transformation.

An Undignified Response and Weapons-grade Prayer

My first gig as a youth pastor was in a church that met in an asbestos hall with no air conditioning. On my first day, I walked in to find my coworker shirtless, wearing board shorts, typing away at a keyboard. Curious about the dress code, I asked, "A little comfortable, aren't we?" In a gentle voice, he replied, "You'll be the same way in about ten minutes."

It was 35 degrees Celsius (95°F) at the end of summer with high humidity and no ventilation. While asbestos isn't flammable, it's remarkably good at trapping heat. Sure enough, ten minutes later, I was shirtless, working alongside him in board shorts. An hour later, the senior pastor walked in, took one look at us, and said, "Let's go to the shops and buy an air conditioner for this room." He also requested we put our shirts back on.

There are two moments in Scripture when worship takes on an undignified posture: when David celebrates the return of the Ark and when a woman anoints Jesus's feet. Even Zacchaeus climbing a tree to see Jesus was, in a way, undignified. My point is that there can be moments of spontaneous, extravagant worship when we set aside formality and allow ourselves to fully express joy and adoration.

In 2 Samuel 6:14–23, David prioritizes joy over reputation when the Ark is returned to Jerusalem. He dances with all his might, caring only about pleasing God, not societal expectations. His surrender isn't about being inappropriate; it's about offering genuine, heartfelt praise. *"I will become even more undignified than this, and I will be humiliated in my own eyes"* (verse 22). God's presence with His people is a cause for celebration, and David dances like no one is watching.

In Luke 7:36–50, a sinful woman anoints Jesus's feet with expensive perfume and wipes them with her hair. That kind of worship is not common today—honestly, I can't recall the last time my feet were washed by a prostitute. The Pharisees are scandalized by this woman's worship, but Jesus honors her extravagant love and faith. She defies social norms to show devotion.

Later, Paul writes in Romans 12:1: *"Therefore, I urge you, brothers and sisters, in view of God's mercy, to offer your bodies as a living sacrifice, holy and pleasing to God—this is your true and proper worship."* Worship isn't just a song or a dance, but a life fully surrendered to God. Psalm 150 describes worship as loud, expressive, and physical—far from the reserved, dignified Sunday service we often expect.

AN UNDIGNIFIED RESPONSE AND WEAPONS-GRADE PRAYER

I wrestle with this in my own faith. I want to be passionate in worship, bold for Christ, and willing to embrace extravagant expressions of devotion. I want to surrender my pride and find humility at the feet of Jesus.

Recently, at a spiritual formation retreat, I grappled with the ideas of desolation and consolation—essentially confronting my deepest sins. It wasn't enjoyable, so I got into my car, blasted two songs, "Chainbreaker" by Zach Williams and "Rattle!" by Elevation Worship, and sang at the top of my lungs. Alone in my car, I had a moment of undignified worship, surrendering my ego and pride.

When we're at a sporting event and our team wins, we scream and celebrate. In 2008, my friends and I watched the Arizona Cardinals play the Pittsburgh Steelers in the Super Bowl. As Kurt Warner made incredible plays, we screamed at the top of our lungs. When we lost, I howled in the backyard. Nothing about that moment was dignified—but we love football. How much more should we be undignified for Jesus?

I often read early church fathers, including Athanasius the Great, Gregory the Theologian, Maximus the Confessor, Seraphim of Sarov, and Theophan the Recluse. I'd love to be known as Duncan the Unpredictable and Undignified, if that meant I cared more about Jesus than my reputation.

Can we bring back old Christian titles?

- Theophan the Recluse
- Symeon the New Theologian
- John the Silent
- Basil the Fool for Christ

- Nilus the Myrrh-Gusher (uncomfortable name, but his relics exuded myrrh)
- Oswald the Generous
- Elizabeth the Wonderworker
- Vincent of Saragossa, the Invincible Martyr
- Alexander the Charcoal Burner

Those are real names. Myrrh-Gusher is a bit much, but the rest are pretty solid. On a Sunday, I'd invite Theophan and John over for a BBQ. Oswald would be great at birthday parties. Elizabeth would be perfect for street evangelism. Alexander? Best guy to have at a BBQ—just get him there early.

When I need undignified worship, I find a raging Pentecostal church. Once in Arizona, I visited a service where a guy with a yarmulke and a ram's horn stood up behind me. The flag-waver had a support crew handing off and folding flags. Three artists painted during worship. A massive gong appeared out of nowhere. Rumor has it, they're still singing the bridge of that song. It was chaotic, undignified, and completely renewing to my soul.

And the prayer—Weapons-Grade Plutonium Prayer. We started praying, and I think we said amen the next day. No order, no preplanned closer—just relentless conversation with Jesus. It was the first time I had to take a bathroom break during prayer. Hours of it—abrasive, overwhelming, and fantastic. One moment, I thought, "Do these Pentecostals even have jobs?" The next moment, I thought, "There's no place I'd rather be." Which, ironically, we may have sung for forty-five minutes straight. In a room like that, there's no ego.

AN UNDIGNIFIED RESPONSE AND WEAPONS-GRADE PRAYER

At the entrance to the gym where I coach, a sign reads: "Leave your shoes and ego at the door. You don't need them on the mats." Leave your shoes and your ego at the door; we don't need them before the Lord. (Unless you've been wearing shoes all day without socks. Then, please, keep them on.) Let's be a little more undignified.

US Camps Are the Best!

I've had the great privilege of being a youth pastor in Australia and in America. The youth camp experience is very different between the two countries. Australian youth camps function like detention centers for international crime lords; concrete block rooms with vinyl beds are the order of the day. Dining rooms are often straight out of 1982, and when you find a good campsite, the level of service soars all the way to four stars.

They're not terrible. I loved Australian camps; they are filled with rustic charm and spiders the size of dinner plates. My conversion story happened on a youth camp, so they hold a special place in my heart. In our Church of Christ movement, we have an amazing campsite where we hold activities in beautiful open spaces. The rooms are excellent, and the food is equally good. This brilliant campsite wasn't typical though as a Christian campsite in Australia.

One time we were taking a crew of kids up the coast of Queensland to the Whitsunday Islands. We stopped in a small country town, and the local youth group put us up in their church. We had sixty-five kids, one toilet, and a hose for a shower. One of the guys was a professional roo shooter. In Australia, kangaroos are like giant mice; when the farms become overpopulated, you have to shoot them.

So, we loaded up in the back of his ute (utility vehicle) and took off through a field. My command was simple. Put a light on a kangaroo, and I send it to be with Jesus. Our professional roo shooter was a twenty-two-year-old man who had a thick Australian accent. In the back of a bouncy truck, he was ready to unleash an apocalypse on the kangaroos as we raced across the field. Every roo that our team put a spotlight on was no more; there must have been a hundred of them. Later that evening, we had delicious kangaroo, which we had humanely hunted in local fields.

When I moved to the States, I went on several youth camp outings. We went to a Young Life campsite in Williams, Arizona, which was basically a community retreat center for millionaires. That was utterly the fanciest camp I have ever been to. There were flying foxes, blobs, cabins, and a dining room hall that featured deer antlers and a giant stuffed bear, which was much bigger than the Koalas I was used to. Just about every activity under the sun was available.

One summer we headed off to San Bernardino Valley, California, and went to the Billy Graham Youth Campsite. This was by far the greatest campsite I'd ever seen; it had a stunning array of activities and structures to use. However, it didn't have rustic charm. It was excellent, and the service was awesome, it had all the charm of a high-end wilderness retreat center. It was the kind of place where you could imagine being invited out to a cabana overlooking the lake and fed daquiris, or to a late afternoon Scandinavian massage. It was a little too nice, neat, and clean—like the woodlands part of Disney World. It was brilliant, but it was missing something.

There is something about a camp experience that should feel different. I'm thankful for good food and excellent speakers. I loved the fact the campsite had a massive lake and inflatable blob, but it was like a resort. Part of me hungered for the students to have the rustic farm experience, sleeping on triple bunks that had vinyl mattresses. Just one time, I wanted a racoon to run wild through a bedroom or someone to get chased by a black bear—not to get mauled, but just to have an incredible cool story to share for the rest of their lives.

I mention this because I wonder whether in our effort to become completely risk adverse, we've surrendered the power of resilience. When a camp has more activities than a high-end amusement park, have we crowded out spaces for honest simple creativity?

Let me put this another way. In the city when you stare at the night sky, you see a few stars dotting the sky. The reason why the sky looks so bleak is light pollution. Most cities have millions of lights that help to light communities and provide safety. Crime drops when communities are well lit. When you get into the country, away from major cities, the sky comes alive. Where there is little or no light pollution, we see millions of stars. It is breath-taking.

In the city you can go an entire lifetime, assuming the couple of hundred stars you see on a particularly dark night is a brilliant sky. Light pollution has robbed you of the full effect of this most extraordinary gift. For eons, weary travelers would peer toward the sky and behold a spectacular show every night, and the sky would come alive with wonder. As cities grew and light pollution increased, the wonder of the night sky was crowded out by streetlamps, skyscrapers, and residential lights. Where we used to look at the beauty of the sky, we now stare at a cityscape and think it's pretty.

What if our youth need the same kind of experiential exchange. The deafening noise of screens and overstimulation has left our God-given creativity starved. We have become oblivious to the creative wonders that have been superseded by a never-ending barrage of activities. I wonder if a student might have a much more profound encounter with God in a monastery, free of technology, learning slow and silent rather than in a noisy and overstimulated environment.

Don't rule out the epic youth camp but add the simple rustic Jesus experience to the mix. When I lived in the States, I would take a two-day sabbatical to a monastery up in Cottonwood, Arizona each year. I'd check in quietly; my meals would be served at the appointed times, but I didn't see another living soul during my stay. The highlight of this campsite was a solitary aquifer where the fish would eat the dead skin off your body when you went for a swim.

The first time I went, I was bored out of my mind. I felt the need to do more and more. I kept telling myself, "I'm going to read and write so much that it's going to be epic." It was free of distractions, and I got a lot of reading and writing done. The second time I headed up, my goal was to sit silently and wait upon the Lord. One might call that a silence and solitude retreat. On that trip, I felt more connected to the presence of God than I had ever before. It was as though the light pollution of my heart had been switched off and for the first time, I could behold God in all his glory.

The shift from doing to being in the presence of God was a revelation. When I cut ties with distractions and activities and just sat and contemplated, I felt something come to life that had been sitting beyond all the pollution in my life. It may be that the best experience we could possibly have with Jesus requires far less, rather than more. We need time to discover that there are astonishing vistas and landscapes singing the tune of Yahweh if we are just willing to stop and observe. In silence, we may discover that the fullness of our prayers is found in learning the art of listening as much as speaking to God.

I am partial to being alone; a cheeky bushwalk or a solo beach run allows me to sit silently and stare into God's creation. No agenda, just there for the view and whatever you want to reveal. Sometimes, that may be something, and other times it's nothing. Either way I take it as a chance to sit in God's good company.

One of the highlights of my student life was our Year 10 Camp. On the last night we did something called a twenty-four-hour solo. We were dropped off at random spots (random to us) along the foreshore of a river. We were given a tarpaulin and a sleeping bag, along with a twenty-four-hour ration pack. They also gave us one book, the Bible. Initially I tried making a spear and hunting bush turkeys; then I attempted to fashion a comfy bed, which turned out to have a small community of ants living in leaf litter. Eventually though, life settled down; the distractions disappeared, and I just started reading for the first time without interruptions. It was fantastic.

After twenty-four hours, I was picked up in a dinghy, and we drove around collecting everyone else. As we rounded the final bend, we saw one of my classmates standing on a rock outcrop in his underpants yelling at a tree. Up the tree was a rather large goanna, with a rope around its neck, attached also to the tarpaulin and his bag of clothes. Turned out it's harder to catch a five-foot lizard than one might think. Either way, that person had sat in his underwear with a meal and a Bible for twenty-four hours. On the journey back to shore, while he was still sitting there in his underpants, he shared just how much fun it was being partially naked, alone, and in solitude.

These days, it takes less to encounter God. For the most part, God is partially obstructed by the light pollution of our lives. To connect in worship, we need less noise, less production, less machine-generated smoke, and fewer light shows. As we seek to create a counter-cultural environment, we should learn to slow down, do less, and create space to encounter God.

A Mighty Red Gum of Faith

There are times when we invest a great deal of emotional and physical energy into activities only to have them fail. The plan was good; the preparation was good. We even prayed into it and felt a confirmation that this was completely the right initiative. We even had close buddies who confirmed the decision every step of the way. Rowan Williams says, "Faith is not the suspension of critical thought, but the decision to trust God's promise and risk living accordingly."[31] Sometimes, we make the decision to risk living accordingly, but the end result doesn't seem to align with what we hoped God's best plan was for our life.

In 2013, I moved back to Australia to plant a church. By that time, I had done three church-planting assessments. I felt pretty darn sure it was the right thing to do. In the buildup to moving from Arizona back to Australia, I had interviewed for a couple of positions at large churches in Phoenix. I turned down all of them to move my family back home to start a church. We had a couple of key partnerships, and fundraising hadn't gone quite as well as I had hoped, but I was prayerfully convinced it was the right thing to do.

The next eighteen months were an unmitigated disaster. We struggled to build a core team; we struggled to build connections; we struggled every Sunday to build a little community and birth a new church. The first Sunday we opened doors, the US church for which we were named had a massive scandal with the lead pastor. Although nobody in our community knew what was going on, part of our hopes for support dried up in an instant.

> *Consider what God has done: Who can straighten what he has made crooked?*
> —Ecclesiastes 7:13

My coaching calls to the US became steadily more frustrating; each time I was reminded how poorly I was doing, and eventually all the support dried up. Our small team, whom I still adore, started to lose confidence; at the same time my father discovered he had cancer and began treatment. I lamented the move back to Australia. Eventually, after all the support and coaching dried up, we decided to close the church. Two years back in Australia and everything I had put my hand to had failed disastrously.

For our final Sunday, we paid good money to book a local worship band, City Alight, in hopes of having an epic worship Sunday. We had twelve people that final Sunday, and two of those were the band. Four were my family, and six were our beautiful little core team, getting ready to say farewell to the project.

I was thirty-five years old and back in Australia, and I felt like every bit of the past seven years had been completely pointless. The move back to Australia was good for the family, and it was great to be around our extended family again, but I was gutted, sad, and frustrated with the Lord over what happened. There were nights when I asked myself why I didn't take the job at the mega-church. They had offered a good salary, an amazing team, and huge vision, and I could have had job security. Instead, I had gone all-in on a decision that ended in a flaming heap.

John 15 is the chapter of Scripture that talks about the vine and says that we are called to abide in Jesus. It's an old idea of trellis—that we are being grafted into Jesus and growing along a trellis. It means that there are healthy vines that might not work into the trellis. They aren't sick, broken, or bad, but they are in the wrong place. The Good Lord prunes those branches to help us redirect our energies into things that are better. Good healthy vines in the wrong place are trimmed so that good healthy vines in the right place can flourish.

I'm a doer, and I like to solve problems. If someone is sharing a problem, I'm not listening for the sake of listening. I'm looking and actively thinking for a resolution. It's the same in the ministry. If something is broken, I'm keen to fix it. If something doesn't work, then let's shut it down and pivot into something else. I'm trying to do the right thing, mixed with the right-now thing.

Max Lucado says, "Faith is not the belief that God will do what you want. It is the belief that God will do what is right."[32] So, what if the right thing is to wait? What if the lesson is about listening to the problem and being empathetic? What if the solution to our giant doing conundrum has more to do with learning through significant failure? Not solving the problem but listening into what might be the godly right thing?

I did a spiritual formation retreat focused on discernment a little while ago. One day, I packed up my journal and passage and went on a bushwalk. The trail was supposed to be easy, but it was basically straight up a ridge incline. About halfway up, I was pleading with the Lord to take the lead or call me home. I was attempting to just listen for God—no agenda but rather just patiently wait upon the Lord. Hot and exhausted, I reached a junction in the road, which was also the peak of the walk. In one direction, the trail wrapped a further five kilometers down to the water. In the other direction was another trail that followed the ridge to another spot. I had about twenty minutes until lunch and sat pondering what I was supposed to do.

I was staring at a gorgeous red gum tree; it was old and had a massive burl where a limb had been sawn off. Branches moved out of it left and right in gnarled forms, and it sat at the corner of the junction in the trail. It was a magnificent tree, towering above the trees around it, but not out of place. It was almost like a confidence building reminder about staying the course and longevity.

I felt like something was being taught in that moment. First, the branches were growing unpredictably. Remember that passage about what God makes crooked. Despite their unpredictability, the trees had grown their branches with purpose. Each of those healthy limbs was allowing the tree to grow bigger and stronger. Second, the branches that were dead or sawn off had not hindered the tree. The tree had grown burls and knots to strengthen those areas, but despite some old wounds, the tree was still immense and healthy.

Later that week I had a prayer meeting with some of the other churches in our area, and one of the pastors shared a vision. He said that sometimes God prunes healthy branches, but that is part of healthy faith. That is, part of the lessons of faith is accepting the failure or loss and learning through those seasons. He added that the pruning hasn't stopped you from being healthy. He had no clue about the red-gum teaching moment I had just had. I got goosebumps. Sometimes, a good limb gets sawn off, and it grows our faith.

When our church plant failed, it opened the door for me to get into breakfast radio. I didn't see it at the time; it took almost another eighteen months before it happened. One opportunity that was trimmed became another opportunity for me to flourish.

My biggest challenge was dealing with the fear of loss. Failure can feel like a big menacing beast until you come face-to-face with it. When that happens suddenly, you realize it wasn't a lion roaring behind the door of failure, but a small Pomeranian making a loud noise. The good thing, the church plant thing, the prayerful and what felt like God-ordained thing was just in the wrong time, wrong season. The lessons from that loss were preparing me for the next five years of breakfast radio.

Later, on the same trail walk, I came across another large red gum tree—one that was dead. I felt a prompting from the Lord. Even in death, there is legacy. This grand old tree reminded me that for countless decades, this tree was growing healthily and when it died it still spoke as a testimony to a life well-lived. You could see the places where branches had been removed, and clearly the tree had grown to a significant size. As I looked at what was left, I could glean little insights into the story of the trees. I felt a prompting: If there is a forest of faith, growth to become big red gum trees requires lessons in pain and loss.

The Slow Messy Grace of Jesus

Jesus obviously moved in the perfect way to accomplish His mission. There can be no doubt that everything Jesus does has purpose and speaks to His reconciling mission for the world. For a moment, imagine that we are a senior marketing team tasked with having maximum impact for Jesus over three years of ministry. What would we do differently to ensure that there could be no doubt that Jesus is who He says He is?

Taking a strictly pragmatic approach, I think my recommendations to Jesus would be vastly different from the plan He used. Here's my take on Ministry Marketing Brief One:

- **Show of Force:** Let's storm the capital with a legion of angels. Overthrow the powers that be and topple the powers and principalities. Jesus, we need you front and center for this operation. This should help to strengthen ties with the religious ruling sect and demonstrate that you sit in the line of David.

- **Big Miracles all the Time:** OK . . . water into wine is a strong opening, but the message is hidden. When we hit miracles, Jesus, they need to be big, bold, public statement pieces. People have short-term memories, so we need to follow up the show of force with some kind of ongoing demonstration of power. Our public performances need to be an overt explanation and demonstration of who you are.
- **Sermon on the Mount with Pizzazz:** Love the talk, but it has a slow opening. We read a lot about the angels encircling Yahweh, but could we get a musical opening from them? Can we get some stone writers on standby, so we can document the performance. There's a lot of mixed meaning here, Lord; let's make it super transparent and ensure that doubters become believers.
- **Disciple Choice:** Years from now, Jesus, they'll make a movie called the *X-Men*. What if we adopted a similar kind of approach—twelve guys, all with some degree of superpowers, maybe make them glow in the dark. Either way, we gotta add some hot sauce to the disciple equation to ensure that everybody knows when they speak, they represent you. Years from now, we'll have a class action lawsuit against Marvel to prove that your disciples were the original X-Men, and that Stan Lee ripped off the idea from you.
- **Everlasting Documentation:** Can we move this beyond spoken word? Jesus, you literally invented the periodic table of elements, so pick a substance that will last for eternity, and let's write this down! I'm talking about

some mylar, type noncombustible, tungsten-grade documentation! People are going to argue over the historicity of what you say. We need to get this down and then get it into proper storage containers!

Even typing that felt wrong. Pomp and performance were never the point of Jesus. Consider this: When the ten heard about the special request from James and John's mother, they were indignant with the two brothers. Jesus called them together and said:

> *You know that the rulers of the Gentiles lord it over them, and their high officials exercise authority over them. Not so with you. Instead, whoever wants to become great among you must be your servant, and whoever wants to be first must be your slave— just as the Son of Man did not come to be served, but to serve, and to give his life as a ransom for many.*
> —Matthew 20:25–28

Jesus moves in an altogether slower and more methodical way. Reading through the accounts, there was permission for his disciples to make mistakes and learn and grow in their faith. At no point did Jesus move toward liberalism, accepting their sins, but He continually looked toward who they could become if their faith, love, and hope grew.

Working on the fringes with ordinary people in extraordinary ways, Jesus moved slowly and with purpose. His methodical pace allowed interruptions (some welcomed, some not), each one providing an opportunity to teach and expand individuals' understanding of who Jesus claimed to be. Jesus rested and slept and ate. The point was a slow, messy gracious demonstration of Jesus's authority that allowed a person to catch up and marvel at what was happening. We see Jesus walking with His disciples, chatting with a woman at the well; each encounter is not rushed or hurried, which allows Christ to be fully present and invested into the life of the individual who is receiving revelation.

This isn't a performance piece. Jesus isn't in the business of making polished saints, and yet He is sanctifying them every step of the way. Everyone is welcome to come as they are, but nobody is welcomed to stay as they are. Each person is called into the transformative work of Jesus—not polished saints, but humble, stumbling saints-in-process. Even Saul, who becomes Paul, is a work-in-progress; there is a radical transformation at his encounter of Jesus from persecutor to great evangelist. At no point does Paul think he has made it to polished perfection. He longs for eternity where that will happen. Aware of the burdens of being an apostle in Christ, he explains this to the Corinthian Church:

> *We are fools for Christ, but you are so wise in Christ! We are weak, but you are strong! You are honored, we are dishonored! To this very hour we go hungry and thirsty, we are in rags, we are brutally treated, we are homeless. We work hard with our own hands. When we are cursed, we bless; when we are persecuted, we endure it; when we are slandered, we answer kindly. We have become the scum of the earth, the garbage of the world—right up to this moment.*
>
> —1 Corinthians 4:10–13

Our posture if we are to be sent ones of Jesus (apostles) is to become followers of Christ, not to perform a spectacle to the wonders of Christ. This isn't about an entertainment venue or performance theater, rather, it is a move of people transformed by an encounter with Jesus and living in an altogether radical way.

I sometimes wonder whether our disillusionment with church grows out of frustration that our manufactured services are giving a Jesus hit, rather than an ongoing transformative effect. We are creating a person who wants a once-a-week event to motivate them like a Tony Robbins motivational talk. That isn't how Jesus leads. Jesus is breaking bread, feeding people, healing people, and sitting with people and ministering. This isn't a dig at the event, but it's a curious wondering about what could be.

> *This is what the L*ORD *says: "Stand at the crossroads and look; ask for the ancient paths, ask where the good way is, and walk in it, and you will find rest for your souls."*
>
> —Jeremiah 6:16

I sometimes think that we are standing at a crossroads, wondering how to connect with a world about the marvels and mysteries of Jesus. On one hand, we have the heritage of the last 300 years of Methodist/Lutheran church style. On the other hand, we have a more ancient way leading to rest for our souls. In the previous Scripture citation, I omitted the last part of Jeremiah 6:16. The verse ends with this: *"But you said, 'We will not walk in it.'"*

I'd hate for us to repeat history and just push back into the path of performance-driven church and miss the call to a non-anxious, peace-driven approach to Jesus—one that echoes the velocity and presence that Jesus has with his disciples. I'm not campaigning for mega-churches or micro churches; I'm campaigning for a shift in speed, one in which Sundays are rejuvenating for everyone, not demoralizing for the staff who put on the show. I want to see a church environment in which healthy leaders are not burning out but growing and championing healthy peace-filled communities.

Let's walk into those ancient paths and not repeat the mistakes of the past.

A Black Sheep Church

I want to float an idea for the framework of evangelism through the lens of church. In Acts 2:42–47, we see a clear model for church:

> *They devoted themselves to the apostles' teaching and to the fellowship, to the breaking of bread and to prayer. Everyone was filled with awe, and many wonders and miraculous signs were done by the apostles. All the believers were together and had everything in common. They sold property and possessions to give to anyone who had need. Every day they continued to meet together in the temple courts. They broke bread in their homes and ate together with glad and sincere hearts, praising God and enjoying the favor of all the people. And the Lord added to their number daily those who were being saved.*

This becomes a model for us to frame up ministry and church on a Sunday, including a clear explanation of sacrament and markers by which we could establish a church. This is a healthy model for fellowship and a good basis for building a solid Jesus-centered church. This is how believers should function. I wonder though if we missed a key point that Jesus makes in the Sermon on the Mount: Who are the people that we want in our churches? More specifically, who is the person that Jesus wants to save? Jesus gives us a framework in Matthew 5:3–10:

> *Blessed are the poor in spirit,*
>   *for theirs is the kingdom of heaven.*
> *Blessed are those who mourn,*
>   *for they will be comforted.*
> *Blessed are the meek,*
>   *for they will inherit the earth.*
> *Blessed are those who hunger and thirst for righteousness,*
>   *for they will be filled.*
> *Blessed are the merciful,*
>   *for they will be shown mercy.*
> *Blessed are the pure in heart,*
>   *for they will see God.*
> *Blessed are the peacemakers,*
>   *for they will be called sons of God.*
> *Blessed are those who are persecuted because of righteousness,*
>   *for theirs is the kingdom of heaven.*

Notice that the people who find the blessings of Jesus are those who are poor, mourning, meek, hungry for righteousness, merciful, pure in heart, and peacemakers. Our marketing departments might have some pushback with Jesus. This is literally how He builds His foundation for new ministry: fishermen, tax collectors, prostitutes, and sinners. These are His starting five for His all-star Jesus team.

His is not a permissive, liberal descent that compromises the heart of the gospel, but a consistent redemptive and edifying model that finds renewal at His feet. Our guiding principle for grace is love, and love actually has boundaries. Christ has accountability, reconciliation, and correction built into His model for church. He marries the truth in love.

Acts 2 is how the believers function, but our connection to culture and community is identifying those who thirst for Jesus and sharing the good news. We push people into an Acts 2 relationships, but I think a church needs to have a black sheep principle based on the beatitudes. We are humble, knowing we've messed up, but we are in the process of being made whole. Slowly walking, we make space and welcome people on the edge.

From the beatitudes, we can infer that Jesus doesn't bench a person in church until they know all the rules. In the beatitudes, they are fully embraced into fellowship. Jesus isn't asking them to spectate but to participate in Church. Let me use this example, if Elton John started attending church tomorrow, I'd hope to have him playing piano within a couple of weeks. The point being participation. Having Elton there on Sunday wouldn't be about pushing a rainbow agenda by wholeheartedly encouraging him to explore who Christ is and how many ways he can be impacted by the good news of Jesus.

Clearly Elton John is talented, and my hope is that connecting him with the worship team would allow him to use that God-given talent in an extraordinary way within the boundaries of our church. I have no doubt it would lead to some messy conversations in our network of churches. But I'd prefer to slowly walk with a black sheep than require everyone to behave before they believe or belong. I wonder if part of the problem is that we've got insanely talented individuals sitting on the sidelines because they just aren't there yet. But they are there . . . sitting . . . waiting.

My biggest jump in capacity as a leader has always come when someone put me into a position **before** others believed I was ready. When I did my first radio show on air, I was a completely new radio talent. Many hosts from other shows tuned in to hear a garbage fire erupt on air. But it was a great show—far better than anyone was expecting. My production director called me into his office to say that some of the other radio show directors had listened and were shocked that I was way better than expected. Confidence-building encouragement helped me rise.

I found myself as an executive pastor before others thought I was ready. I found myself as a lead pastor when others doubted my ability. I wrote books when people told me I was terrible at writing. I competed at the US Open in Jiu Jitsu before I felt like I had the capacity. Some of those moments like the Jiu Jitsu tournament led to crushing defeats. However, in each moment, my confidence accelerated my capacity, and I grew as a person. In each case I was allowed to fail, but in each case, I needed to learn.

Velocity is the main thing when we consider the difference between desolation and consolation. Whereas we are driven to desolation by quick unsustainable movement, we are drawn to consolation by a slower and more gracious pace. Consolation is the wavelength on which Jesus is moving. The velocity that we see in the modern church where people find themselves burned out is a driving force, not a drawing force. Modern church planners want us to move in a straight line, drive on a highway of discipleship that moves way too quickly. Our faith is not formed in a linear manner; rather, the journey has twists turns and bumps. A black sheep church allows us to pivot or change direction and adapt as circumstances change, but the goal remains the same. Resilience is found in hardship and sufferings.

> *But he said to me, "My grace is sufficient for you, for my power is made perfect in weakness." Therefore I will boast all the more gladly about my weaknesses, so that Christ's power may rest on me. That is why, for Christ's sake, I delight in weaknesses, in insults, in hardships, in persecutions, in difficulties. For when I am weak, then I am strong.*
> —2 Corinthians 12:9–10

If our expectation is sufficiency of grace where God power is proclaimed in weakness, we might have found an ancient path. Our weakness is Christ's strength, and it should be the hallmark of a black sheep church. As I reflect on our church, I admit that we aren't the best at anything. Our worship is OK; my preaching is OK; our marketing is way below par. A bunch of things aren't our strong suit (my leadership might be listed here). But the thing I love about our church is our passion for making people welcome and allowing them space to encounter Jesus. Our pace isn't quick, but sometimes slow is lasting. Jesus works slowly, and the fruit endures forever.

Closing Thoughts

Sometimes, the last chapter of a book is written to bring together all the previous ideas in the one glorious bow. However, this book was designed to be a collection of thoughts and funny stories; it is not intended to fix anything or wrap things up neatly into a little bow. It's a thought-starter, like we're peeking into the upper room and asking, "Come, Lord Jesus, walk with us again."

I've been wrestling through this idea of liminality. *Liminality*, which means "being in between," describes the state of being in a transitional phase or on the edge of something new, often characterized by ambiguity and disorientation. If you are feeling ambiguous about the church or disoriented because of the season we've just come out of, you aren't alone. The thing about these kinds of seasons is that they may spark creative explosions that lead toward profound change.

More and more, I find it easy to share my faith and love for Jesus. Brazilian Jiu Jitsu has been the face of that in recent years, and I honed my ability to share my faith by doing breakfast radio. A curious thing happens when you have permission to speak into a person's safe space about the Good News of Jesus. In your car, you are alone, and it is your safe space. I know this because my guess is like me, you occasionally fart in a car when you are alone. Crude.

After five years of letting down my guard on radio and sharing my life and story of faith, I realized that the success of the show I did with Sam Robinson (not related) lay in our ability to talk with ease about our faith along with everything else. We could jump from the weather to movies to a funny phone call segment and then slide into conversations about faith. It felt effortless. When we did this and the message of Jesus was shared (while your guard is down in the car), we saw profound impacts.

When authenticity and honesty become pillars for the next season of the church, grace can become the engine for our faith, expanding with the goal of drawing people into a deeper relationship with Jesus. Imagine the moment in the upper room when Jesus feasted with His disciples. They are His friends; there is laughter and sharing, but ahead is the hardest journey of Jesus's life. In that room are the last moments He can pour into His friends. Jesus takes those moments to share food with them and impart some final pieces of wisdom before His hour draws near.

In John 14 Jesus not only comforts His disciples but promises the Holy Spirit to lead and guide them. His compassion and grace for His community are on display, and soon the Holy Spirit will be imparted to the people of God creating a bond of unhindered intimacy. We become the temples; the Good Lord is no more than twelve inches away from our heads in our hearts.

CLOSING THOUGHTS

What if we end with this idea of an invitation to the upper room—a metaphorical call to deeper spiritual intimacy and an expectation of encounter with God. This is a call to a space where we seek guidance, renewal, and a deeper connection with God—where we desire most deeply to seek God's presence in our lives and where our weaknesses are filled with the strength of God. In this space, we slowly discern God's will at the speed of Jesus, and we consciously and regularly pull away from lifestyle distractions to linger a little longer in the upper room with God.

Endnotes

1. Bob Goff, *Love Does: Discover a Secretly Incredible Life in an Ordinary World* (Thomas Nelson, 2012), 15.

2. N. T. Wright, *God and the Pandemic: A Christian Reflection on the Coronavirus and Its Aftermath* (Zondervan, 2020), Kindle.

3. Cyrian, *On the Unity of the Church* (Latin: De Ecclesiae Catholicae Unitate), section 6. https://christianhistoryinstitute.org/study/module/cyprian.

4. Abraham Joshua Heschel, *The Sabbath* (Farrar Straus Giroux, 1951), vii–xvi.

5. Heschel, *The Sabbath*, xiv.

6. Heschel, *The Sabbath*, xiv.

7. Heschel, *The Sabbath*, 101.

8. Brennan Manning, *The Ragamuffin Gospel: Good News for the Bedraggled, Beat-Up, and Burnt Out,* (Multnomah Books, 2000), 22.

9. Martin Seligman, *Learned Optimism: How to Change Your Mind and Your Life* (Vintage, 2006), Kindle.

10. Pope Francis, "Pope Warns of Social Media Perils: Relationships Reduced to Algorithms, Partisan Propaganda, Hatred," *AP News*, August 26, 2023, https://apnews.com/article/pope-vatican-social-media-propaganda-technocracy-d1642396fb0c09b34af5fcca31b287b6.

11 Daria J. Kuss and Mark D. Griffith, "Social Networking Sites and Addiction: Ten Lessons Learned," *International Journal of Environmental Research and Public Health* 12, no. 3 (2017), 311, https://doi.org/10.3390/ijerph120201286.

12 Lawrence T. Lam and Zi-Wen Peng, "Effect of Pathological Use of the Internet on Adolescent Mental Health: A Prospective Study," *Archives of Pediatrics & Adolescent Medicine*, 164 no. 10 (2010), 901–906. https://doi.org/10.1001/archpediatrics.2010.159.

13 Anna Vannucci, Kaitlin M. Flannery, and Christine McCauley Ohannessian, "Social Media Use and Anxiety in Emerging Adults," *Depression and Anxiety* 33, no. 7 (2017), 611–618, https://doi.org/10.1002/da.22466.

14 Louis Leung and Paul S. N. Lee, "Impact of Internet Literacy, Internet Addiction Symptoms, and Internet Activities on Academic Performance," *Social Science Computer Review* 30, no. 4, (2012), 403–418, https://doi.org/10.1177/0894439311435217.

15 Mark Sayers, *A Non-Anxious Presence: How a Changing and Complex World Will Create a Remnant of Renewed Christian Leaders* (Moody Publishers, 2022).

16 John Mark Comer, *Practicing the Way: Be with Jesus. Become Like Him. Do As He Did* (WaterBrook, 2024), xiii.

17 Comer, *The Ruthless Elimination of Hurry: How to Stay Emotionally Healthy and Spiritually Alive in the Chaos of the Modern World* (WaterBrook, 2019), Kindle.

18 Francois Fénelon, *Maxims of the Saints*, https://ccel.org/ccel/fenelon/maxims/maxims.ii.html, Article Third.

19 Saint Teresa of Avila, https://www.goodreads.com/author/quotes/74226.Teresa_de_vila.

20 Jurgen Moltmann, *Theology of Hope: On the Ground and the Implications of a Christian Eschatology* (SCM Press, 1967).

21 N. T. Wright, *Surprised by Hope: Rethinking Heaven, the Resurrection, and the Mission of the Church* (HaperOne, 2008), 234.

22 Timothy Keller, *The Reason for God: Belief in an Age of Skepticism* (Penguin, 2009), 212.

23 Kevin J. Vanhoozer, *The Drama of Doctrine: A Canonical Linguistic Approach to Christian Theology* (Westminster John Knox Press, 2005).

24 Gerald O'Collins, *The Resurrection of Jesus Christ* (Judson Press, 1973), 134.

25 Tony Campolo, "The Church Is a Whore," YouTube, https://www.youtube.com/watch?v=PM_XY7JlG5Y.

26 Augustine, *Sermones post Maurinos reperti in Miscellanea Agostiniana*, vol. 1, ed. G. Morin, 1930, 447.

27 Jack Reese, *At the Blue Hole: Elegy for a Church on the Edge* (Eerdmans, 2021).

28 Adapted from Loren Eiseley, "The Star Thrower," originally published in *The Unexpected Universe* (Harcourt Brace Jovanovich, 1969).

29 Evagrius Ponticus, *The Praktikos: Chapters on Prayer, (Volume 4)*, trans. John Eudes Bamberger (Cistercian Publications, 1972).

30 James Clear, *Habits: An Easy and Proven Way to Build Good Habits and Break Bad Ones* (Avery, 2018).

31 Rowan Williams, *Tokens of Trust: An Introduction to Christian Belief* (Westminster John Knox Press, 2007), 45.

32 Max Lucado, *He Still Moves Stones: Everyone Needs a Miracle* (W Pub Group,1993), Kindle.

www.ingramcontent.com/pod-product-compliance
Lightning Source LLC
LaVergne TN
LVHW051059080426
835508LV00019B/1958